More Praise for *Student-Centered Leadership*

"No one has conducted a more thorough and deeply insightful examination of the role of school leaders than Viviane Robinson. *Student-Centered Leadership* shines with clarity and practical, powerful ideas. Three big capabilities and five key dimensions provide a comprehensive and accessible framework for any leader or those working with leaders. Add this book to your leadership library."

—Michael Fullan, author, *The Six Secrets of Change* and *Leading in a Culture of Change*

"Viviane Robinson's book brings a new level of precision to the whole idea of instructional leadership. Her incisive and tough-minded approach also has many wise and practical ideas for leading schools that truly focus on students' learning. This is a book all leaders can and should use!"

—Ben Levin, Canada Research Chair, OISE/University of Toronto

"If you're seeking an up-to-date, solidly researched, practical resource for understanding how leadership makes a difference in schools, look no further."

—Phil Hallinger, Joseph Lau Chair Professor of Leadership and Change, Institute of Education, Hong Kong

"How refreshing it is to read a book on leadership that moves us away from rhetoric and empty clichés toward the actual behaviors and strategies that can be used to improve outcomes for students. Viviane Robinson's compelling book is both evidence based and profoundly practical. *Student-Centered Leadership* is a must-read for school leaders who want to make a greater difference."

—Steve Munby, chief executive, National College for Leadership of Schools and Children's Services, England

"Viviane Robinson's experience in bringing research to bear on problems of school development and leadership is reflected in every chapter of this book. I found her highly readable synthesis a motivating counterpoint both to dense leadership texts and frothy summaries. It will be an equally important resource for individual school leaders, professional developers, and administrator-preparation programs. There will be two copies on my shelf—one to loan and one for my own reference."

—Karen Seashore Louis, Regents Professor,
University of Minnesota

"A must-read for school leaders and those who work with them! Grounded in the best available evidence, this book provides useful and usable knowledge about the practical aspects of school leadership. Avoiding faddism, Robinson defines and develops the five dimensions of school leadership, carefully and cogently making the case for each and its relation to improving student learning."

—Jim Spillane, Spencer T. and Ann W. Olin
Professor in Learning and Organizational Change,
Northwestern University

"To read this book is to meet Viviane Robinson, an energetic, passionate practitioner focused on what works. She engages and inspires readers with something for the *head*—rigorous, evidence-based research, the *heart*—a focus on the leader's moral purpose to make a positive and lasting difference in the lives of young people, and *hands*—a call to action and influence in schools that will optimize impact. This text will top the list of my recommendations to leaders both experienced and aspiring."

—Bruce Armstrong, director, Bastow Institute
of Educational Leadership, Victoria, Australia

Student-Centered Leadership

THE JOSSEY-BASS

Leadership Library in Education

•

Andy Hargreaves

Consulting Editor

THE JOSSEY-BASS LEADERSHIP LIBRARY IN EDUCATION is a distinctive series of original, accessible, and concise books designed to address some of the most important challenges facing educational leaders. Its authors are respected thinkers in the field who bring practical wisdom and fresh insight to emerging and enduring issues in educational leadership. Packed with significant research, rich examples, and cutting-edge ideas, these books will help both novice and veteran leaders understand their practice more deeply and make schools better places to learn and work.

ANDY HARGREAVES is the Thomas More Brennan Chair in Education in the Lynch School of Education at Boston College. He is the author of numerous books on culture, change, and leadership in education.

For current and forthcoming titles in the series, please see the last page of this book.

Student-Centered Leadership

Viviane Robinson

JOSSEY-BASS
A Wiley Imprint
www.josseybass.com

Published by Jossey-Bass
A Wiley Imprint
989 Market Street, San Francisco, CA 94103-1741—www.josseybass.com

Jossey-Bass books and products are available through most bookstores. To contact Jossey-Bass directly call our Customer Care Department within the U.S. at 800-956-7739, outside the U.S. at 317-572-3986, or fax 317-572-4002.

Jossey-Bass also publishes its books in a variety of electronic formats. Some content that appears in print may not be available in electronic books.

Library of Congress Cataloging-in-Publication Data

Robinson, V. M. J. (Viviane M. J.)
    Student-centered leadership / Viviane Robinson.—1st ed.
        p. cm.—(Jossey-Bass Leadership library in education)
    Includes bibliographical references and index.
    ISBN 978-0-470-87413-4 (pbk.); ISBN 978-1-118-09027-5 (ebk.);
ISBN 978-1-118-09028-2 (ebk.); ISBN 978-1-118-09029-9 (ebk.)
    1. Educational leadership. I. Title.
    LB2805.R688 2011
    371.2—dc22

                                                                    2011011789

Printed in the United States of America
FIRST EDITION
PB Printing 10 9 8 7 6 5 4 3 2

Contents

Figures and Tables

Figures

Tables

The Author

After completing her doctorate at Harvard University, Viviane Robinson returned to her home country of New Zealand to take up a position at the University of Auckland, where she currently holds a personal chair as professor of education. The hallmark of her career has been serving educational practitioners through research and development that is simultaneously rigorous and relevant to the world of practice. She has pursued this passion through her research on leadership, school improvement, and organizational learning. She is the author of five books and numerous chapters and journal articles. Her work has been published in such leading international journals as *Educational Researcher*, *Educational Administration Quarterly*, and *Review of Educational Research*.

Viviane is also the academic director of the Centre for Educational Leadership in the Faculty of Education. The centre delivers the national induction program for new school principals and a comprehensive suite of research-based professional learning opportunities for all types of school leaders.

Viviane has consulted on leadership development and research for governmental and professional bodies in England, Singapore, Canada, Australia, and New Zealand. She has received awards for her contribution to educational research, policy, and practice in New Zealand, Australia, and the United States. In 2011 she was made a Fellow of the American Educational Research Association.

Acknowledgments

The initial research for this book was completed under a contract with the New Zealand Ministry of Education to write a best evidence synthesis (BES) of research on educational leadership (Robinson, Hohepa, & Lloyd, 2009). I owe a considerable debt of gratitude to Adrienne Alton-Lee, chief education advisor at the Ministry of Education, for initiating and leading the whole BES program and for supporting me throughout the process of completing the leadership BES. The transition from writing the BES to writing this book was made far easier by the feedback I received from hundreds of school and district leaders and graduate students who attended my presentations and workshops and encouraged me to continue this work.

The number of individuals who have shaped my thinking about leadership are far too numerous to name individually. But I would like to acknowledge a huge intellectual debt to Chris Argyris—one of my mentors at Harvard University who encouraged my conviction that the job of educators was to make a better world and taught me how to test the adequacy of my efforts. Everything I have written in this book about relationships is grounded in the values and ethics of his work.

New Zealand and Australian colleagues who contributed directly or indirectly to this book include Margie Hohepa and Claire Lloyd, who worked with me on the original leadership BES, and John Hattie and the late Ken Rowe, who helped with effect size analyses. Discussions over many years with Graeme Aitken about quality teaching helped me enormously with Chapter Five. Claire Sinnema's brilliance in the design of figures and diagrams was invaluable for sharpening and communicating my ideas.

International colleagues have been generous with their time and have given me thoughtful feedback on this work or related manuscripts. I had wonderful discussions with Ken Leithwood about the place of transformational leadership and with Karen Seashore Louis about instructional leadership in a high-stakes policy environment. Karen also introduced me to Mia Urick, professional development director for the Minnesota Association of School Administrators. Mia's enthusiastic feedback about an early draft reassured me about the relevance and importance of the work for a U.S. audience. Conversations with Jim Spillane, Peter Gronn, Alma Harris, and Ellen Goldring helped me stay focused on leadership practices and their development. Kathryn Riley gave me some pertinent feedback on draft sections on engaging the community. Without the generous sabbatical provisions of The University of Auckland this book would not have been completed on time and with enjoyment! Thanks to Peter, Alma, and Jim for providing me with a writing base for part of my sabbatical.

I owe a very special thank you to Darleen Opfer, whose detailed feedback on a near-final draft enabled me to see gaps and inconsistencies I would have otherwise missed. The wise words of the series editor, Andy Hargreaves, at the beginning of the project enabled me to write with passion and freedom while still staying true to my research base.

I have dedicated previous books to my husband, David, and do so again because he continues to be the emotional support and anchor that enables me to take on the challenges I have in the last few years. He has read drafts, cooked the dinner, and picked me up when the going got tough. Thank you.

June 2011   Viviane Robinson
                                               Auckland, New Zealand

The "What" and the "How" of Student-Centered Leadership

Most school leaders are motivated by the desire to make a difference to their students. They want to lift their students' achievement, increase their confidence, and give them opportunities they would never find elsewhere. Although we should admire their moral purpose, fine words and high ideals are not enough. If leaders don't know how to put their words into action, if they follow the wrong paths and take the wrong turns, then their sense of moral purpose can quickly give way to cynicism, frustration, and fading commitment.

This book is not another call to the moral high ground. Most educational leaders are already there or at least want to be. Instead, it is a book about how to turn ideals into action. It provides leaders with guidance about how to make a bigger difference to their students—guidance that is based not on fad or fashion but on the best available evidence about what works for students.

When school leaders reflect on what keeps them in a highly challenging job, they typically describe the difference they make to the lives of children and the difference children make to their own lives. They describe how, on the "horrible days," they get an emotional lift by stopping by classrooms to see children and celebrate their achievements. They believe passionately that "you can't beat working with children." But they are just as aware of the children they have not reached—the children for whom school was a place of failure and humiliation or the children for whom school did make a difference but not enough to overcome the challenges of their family circumstances.

The job of school leadership offers enormous rewards and increasing challenges. My motivation for writing this book is to help school leaders increase the rewards while meeting the challenges by describing, explaining, and illustrating new research evidence about the types of leadership practice that make the biggest difference to the learning and well-being of the students for whom they are responsible.

Leadership in Challenging Times

The expectations for today's school leaders have never been more ambitious. Leaders work in systems that expect schools to enable *all* students to succeed with intellectually challenging curricula. Although no education system in the western world has achieved this goal, and it is not clear how it can be achieved at scale, school leaders are held responsible for making progress toward it. In the United States, under the federal legislation known as No Child Left Behind (NCLB), the accountabilities associated with these policy expectations can be punitive and demoralizing, especially for leaders in schools that serve economically disadvantaged communities (Mintrop & Sunderman, 2009).

These ambitious expectations come at a time when the school population has never been more diverse. This diversity has revealed the limitations of schooling systems that cannot rapidly teach children the cognitive and linguistic skills that enable them to engage successfully with the school curriculum. Because increasing numbers of children arrive at school without these skills, achieving the goal of success for all students may require major changes to business as usual.

On the positive side, these increased expectations have been accompanied by a greater understanding of the importance of leadership for achieving the goal of success for all students. A new wave of research on educational leadership has shown that the quality of leadership can make a substantial difference to the achievement of students, and not just on low-level standardized tests (Robinson, Lloyd, & Rowe, 2008). In schools where students achieve well above expected levels, the leadership looks quite different from the leadership in otherwise similar lower-performing schools. In the higher-performing schools it is much more focused on the business of improving learning and teaching.

There is no doubt that this body of evidence about the links between leadership and student outcomes has been noticed by policy makers and professional associations. It has informed the development of educational leadership standards in the United States (Council of Chief State School Officers, 2008), the work of the National College of School Leadership and Children's Services in England (Leithwood, Day, Sammons, Harris, & Hopkins, 2006), and the development of leadership frameworks in Australia and New Zealand (New Zealand Ministry of Education, 2008). The research has confirmed what school leaders knew all along— that the quality of leadership matters and that it is worth investing in that quality.

Another positive feature of the leadership environment is the shift from an emphasis on leadership style to leadership practices. Leadership styles, such as transformational, transactional, democratic, or authentic leadership, are abstract concepts that tell us little about the behaviors involved and how to learn them. The current emphasis on leadership practices moves leadership away from the categorization of leaders as being of a particular type to a more flexible and inclusive focus on identifying the effects of broad sets of leadership practices. Rather than anxiously wonder about whether you are, for example, a transformational leader, I will be encouraging you to think instead about the frequency and quality in your school of the leadership practices that this new research has shown make a difference to the learning and achievement of students.

What Is Student-Centered Leadership?

In this book, the ruler for judging the effectiveness of educational leadership is its impact on the learning and achievement of students for whom the leader is responsible. Although educators contest the value to be given to particular types of achievement, and argue about whether certain assessments and tests measure what is important, the principle at stake here is willingness to judge educational leadership by its impact on the educational outcomes of students. Do the decisions and actions of the school's leadership improve teaching in ways that are reflected in better student learning, or is their focus so far removed from the classroom that leadership adds little value to student learning?

There are compelling ethical arguments for student-centered leadership. Because the point and purpose of compulsory schooling is to ensure that students learn what society has deemed important, a central duty of school leadership is to create the conditions that make that possible. Although this criterion for leadership effectiveness might seem to some readers to be too narrow, in reality it is not because leaders need to work on so many different fronts to achieve it.

Typically, judgments of leadership effectiveness stop short of asking about effect on student learning. Perhaps the most common approach to judging school leadership is the quality of school management—children are happy and well behaved, the school is orderly, the property is looked after, and the finances are under control. Although high-quality school management represents a considerable achievement, it should not be equated with leadership effectiveness because it is possible for students in well-managed schools to be performing well below their expected level. High-quality management is a necessary but not a sufficient condition for leadership effectiveness because it requires, in addition, that the school's management procedures ensure high-quality teaching and learning. There is a considerable stretch between the two.

A second approach to judging leadership effectiveness is based on the quality of leaders' relationships with the *adults* in the system. Principals who are popular with staff and parents and get along with district officials are judged to be effective. These relationships are important because little can be achieved by school leaders if they alienate their staff, are in constant dispute with district officials, or cannot earn the trust of their communities. But once again, this criterion is not sufficient for judging the effectiveness of school leaders because good relationships with adults do not guarantee a high-quality learning environment for students.

A third unsatisfactory approach to judging leadership effectiveness is to equate it with innovation. Leaders who get on board with the latest innovations in school organization, curriculum, or community outreach often have high profiles and are showcased as effective leaders. But like good staff relationships, innovative practice is not necessarily predictive of student learning. We know that many innovations do not work and that schools engaged in multiple innovations can burn out staff, create incoherence in the instructional program, and actually make things worse for their students (Hess, 1999).

One of the reasons that school management, staff relationships, and innovative practice have overshadowed student impact as the criterion for leadership effectiveness is that it is very difficult to isolate the contribution of leadership to student progress. Except in the smallest of our schools, leaders influence students indirectly by creating the conditions required for teaching and learning. It is easier to create those conditions in schools that enroll students with high levels of prior achievement than it is to create those conditions in schools that enroll students with lower achievement levels. The apparent success of leaders in the first type of school may be more a reflection of the students and of the community from which they are drawn than of the effectiveness of the leadership.

The indirectness of leadership effects on students, plus the confounding influence of factors such as student and community background, make it very difficult to isolate out the contribution of leadership itself. That is probably why leadership effectiveness has been judged by qualities such as staff relationships and degree of innovation—qualities that are assumed to be good for students. In the absence of good evidence, these taken-for-granted assumptions have become substitutes for student-centered measures of leadership effectiveness. In advocating a student-centered approach to leadership effectiveness, I am seeking to disrupt the assumption that what is good for the adults is good for the students and to encourage a more deliberate examination of the relationship between the two.

Whose Leadership?

My answer to this question is that this book is for everyone who exercises leadership in schools. But that answer just raises further questions about what I mean by leadership. And until we sort out what is meant by leadership in this book, I can't answer the question of whom this book is for.

It is commonly asserted that leadership is the exercise of influence, but so is force, coercion, and manipulation, and we wouldn't call those types of influence *leadership*. So there must be something else. Leadership is distinguished from force, coercion, and manipulation by the *source* of the influence. The influence that we associate with leadership comes from three different sources. The first source is the reasonable exercise of formal authority—the critical factor here is that those who are influenced see the use of the authority as reasonable. The principal had a tough decision to make—she explained why she made it, and although we didn't all agree we do understand that a decision had to be made.

A second source of leadership influence is attraction to one or more of the personal qualities of the leader. The leader is admired for his dedication, selflessness, ethic of caring, or courage. This is when character enters the frame—attractive personal qualities increase the chance of being influential with colleagues. A third source of leadership influence is relevant expertise—one gains influence by offering knowledge and skills that help others make progress on the tasks for which they are responsible.

In the following scenario in which a group of teachers meet to review the results of a recent assessment in science, we see the fluid operation of these sources of influence (Robinson, 2001, p. 92):

> *Mary, the head of science, is chairing a meeting in which her staff are reviewing the results of the assessment of the last unit of work. She circulated the results in advance, with notes about how to interpret them, and asked the team to think about their implications for next year's teaching of the unit. The team identifies common misunderstandings and agrees they need to develop resources that help students to overcome them. Julian, a second-year teacher, was pretty unhappy with the assessment protocol used this year and suggests revisions that he thinks will give more recognition to students who have made an extra effort. Most of his suggestions are adopted. Lee, who teaches information technology as well as science, shows the group how the results have been processed on the computer so that they can be combined with other assessments and used in reports to parents and the board. Several team members express nervousness about reporting to the board so they decide to review a draft report at the next meeting.*

Mary, as head of science, influences her colleagues by asking them to prepare for their meeting and structuring the agenda. Despite Julian and Lee having no formal authority, they too influence how the task is done through their ideas about how to improve the assessment and reporting procedures. All three people in this meeting exercised leadership because their authority (in Mary's case) and their ideas changed how the task was done. They moved fluidly between being in the lead and following the lead of others.

So leadership is, by its very nature, not just the purview of those with formal authority over others. One can also lead from a basis of expertise, ideas, and personality or character, and, in principle, these sources of influence are open to anyone. This means that leadership is by its very nature distributed. It follows, therefore, that this book is for all who seek to increase their leadership influence, whether or not they have a formal leadership position.

The "What" and the "How" of Student-Centered Leadership

If student-centered leadership is about making a bigger difference to student learning and well-being, then leaders need trustworthy advice about the types of leadership practice that are most likely to deliver those benefits. This book offers such advice based on a rigorous analysis of all the published evidence about the impact of particular types of leadership practice on a variety of student outcomes.

The first thing I learned in doing the analysis is that of the hundreds of thousands of studies about educational leadership only a minuscule proportion of them have examined the impact of leadership on any sort of student outcome. This, in itself, shows the radical disconnection between research on educational leadership and the core business of teaching and learning. In the end, I found about thirty studies, mostly conducted in the United States, that measured the direct or indirect impact of leadership on student outcomes. In about half of these thirty studies, leadership was measured by asking teachers to complete surveys about the practices of their principal. In the other half, teachers were asked about the leadership of their school. That is why the findings in Figure 1.1 tell us about the impact of school leadership rather than principalship. The student outcome measures were usually about academic achievement (math, literacy, or language arts), though a few studies used measures of social outcomes such as students' participation and engagement in their schooling. The five dimensions presented in Figure 1.1 were derived by listing all the individual survey items that had been used to measure leadership and grouping them into common themes. Once the 199 survey items had been sorted into the final five leadership dimensions, the statistics reported in the original studies were used to calculate an average effect size for each dimension. The effect size statistic alongside each of the horizontal bars indicates the average impact of the leadership dimension on student outcomes. (More details about the methodology of the meta-analysis can be found in Robinson, Lloyd, & Rowe, 2008.)

Our analyses of these studies enabled us to sort the different leadership practices into five broad categories or leadership dimensions. For each dimension, we used the information in

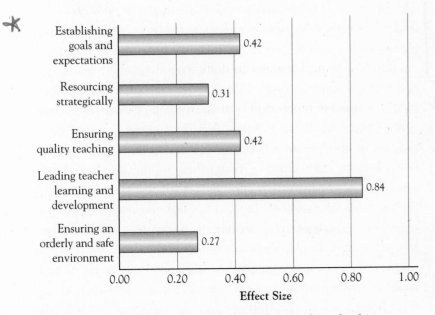

Figure 1.1   Five Dimensions of Student-Centered Leadership
Note: The effect size statistic indicates the average impact of the leadership dimension on student outcomes as calculated from the available published studies (see Robinson, Lloyd, & Rowe, 2008, for further details).

the original studies to calculate its impact on student outcomes. Technical information about how these calculations were performed is available in Robinson, Lloyd, and Rowe (2008).

The average impact of each dimension on student outcomes is represented by the effect size statistic at the end of each horizontal bar in Figure 1.1. Although there are no hard and fast rules about how to interpret this statistic in educational research, an effect of 0.20 is usually considered small, 0.40 a moderate effect, and 0.60 and above a large effect (Hattie, 2009). Given these rough benchmarks, Figure 1.1 presents a very positive story about the contribution leaders can make to the achievement and well-being of their students.

Although I could have ordered the horizontal bars in Figure 1.1 to reflect the relative size of their effects, I have chosen instead to order them in a way that tells a story about their inter-relationships. The story is that student-centered leadership sets clear goals for student learning, provides resources for those goals, and works closely with teachers to plan, coordinate, and monitor how they are achieved. Through such oversight, they are likely to learn that goal achievement requires increased teacher capacity. Leaders' close involvement in building such capacity gives them a clear understanding of the conditions and the support teachers need to learn more effective instructional practice. These four types of leadership are enabled by, and contribute to, an orderly and safe school environment.

The five dimensions work together as a set and have strong reciprocal effects. When, for example, student learning goals are clear, leaders are more likely to discover what teachers need to learn in order to teach their students. When leaders provide high-quality opportunities for teachers to learn those practices, student-learning goals are more likely to be achieved.

Some, if not all, of the five dimensions in Figure 1.1 will be familiar to many readers. After all, the importance of instructional leadership—broadly speaking of leadership that is focused on teaching and learning—has been a recurring theme in recent leadership research and policy thinking. What this book does that is different is to go well beyond the broad idea of instructional leadership to identify and explain specific leadership practices involved in each of the five dimensions so that readers can enhance their understanding and their skills in what I have called *student-centered leadership*. In order to apply the five dimensions wisely in any given context, leaders need to understand why and how the practices involved make a difference to teaching and learning. For that reason I have given considerable emphasis in this book to clearly explaining and richly illustrating the theory and principles that are responsible for these leadership effects. The explanations are based on relevant theories and concepts from business, organizational studies, and social psychology as well as education. For example, in the chapter on goal setting, I draw on the very rich literature from social psychology and organizational studies to explain how goal setting works and the conditions under which it does and does not increase performance. This evidence forms the basis of my discussion of the practicalities of using goal setting in schools, including how to respond to possible objections to its use. The descriptions and explanations of the five dimensions are intended to provide a rich and rigorous . guide to the question, "What practices are involved in student-centered leadership?"

My illustrations of the dimensions include positive and negative examples because I want readers to discriminate the qualities that actually make the difference to student and teacher learning. I want to disrupt the assumption that having a general idea about, for example, goal setting or teacher professional learning is sufficient for effective leadership. There are often subtle but critical qualities that make the difference between whether or not the practice in question will deliver the intended benefits. That is why I spend some time explaining and illustrating what does and does not work. I want readers who have a "general idea" to gain a more precise understanding of the shifts in their practice that will enable them to lead in ways that have a higher probability of enhancing the learning of their teachers and students.

The scope of leadership work is huge, and, not surprisingly, many books on leadership try to match that scope. In writing this book, my personal mantra has been, "a few powerful ideas, clearly explained and richly illustrated." The key ideas I have selected are those that I believe will provide leaders with the understanding they need to adapt the outcomes-linked evidence in Figure 1.1 to their own schools. As I explain in Chapter Six on leading teacher professional learning, we know that professional development by bullet point does not work because it uncouples practical "tips" from the principles that enable practitioners to make the tips work in their own setting. You will find plenty of practical tips in this book, but they will always be linked to evidence and theoretical principles.

The "What" of Student-Centered Leadership: Five Dimensions

The first dimension of student-centered leadership involves establishing goals and expectations. Goal setting is a ubiquitous feature of leadership work. It is part of strategic and annual planning, principal and teacher evaluation, and many other school development and review processes. Yet despite this, much goal setting remains a paper exercise that fails to focus the collective effort of staff on agreed priorities. In Chapter Three, I describe the conditions needed to make goal setting work properly and how to overcome challenges to its use. I explain how, in a world where everything seems important, or at least important to someone, goal setting enables leaders to sort through the multiple demands to establish the *relative* importance of these various demands and thus provide a clear steer for an otherwise rudderless ship. Once clear goals are established, the second dimension of effective leadership—resourcing strategically—comes into play (Chapter Four). Scarce resources—money, time, teaching materials, and instructional expertise—are allocated in ways that give priority to key goals. Staff can see an alignment among school goals, expenditure, and reform initiatives. Efforts to recruit and develop instructional expertise are aligned to the student needs that have shaped current goals.

Strategic resourcing and strategic thinking are closely linked. Strategic thinking involves asking questions and challenging assumptions about the links between resources and the needs they are intended to meet. Too often leaders invest time and energy in an innovation without asking, "What conditions are required to make this resource work for the students in my school?" "What evidence do I have that this type of resource allocation will help me achieve this goal?" Problematic assumptions about the effectiveness of particular types of resourcing are identified throughout this chapter.

The third dimension of student-centered leadership involves ensuring quality teaching through planning, coordinating, and evaluating teachers and their teaching (Chapter Five). The evidence suggests that in schools where teachers report that their leadership is heavily involved in these activities, students do better. This type of leadership is at the heart of what is called *instructional leadership* in the North American literature. The powerful ideas that are discussed in this chapter are program coherence, effective teaching, and creating a culture of inquiry. It is not often that a theory of effective teaching is included in a book on educational leadership, but I believe that because assumptions about effective teaching inform many leadership practices, leaders need an explicit and defensible theory if they are to lead the improvement of teaching and learning.

Strong instructional leadership focused on ambitious learning goals soon uncovers shortfalls in teachers' knowledge and skill. In many cases, those shortfalls are shared by their leaders as well. A powerful difference can be made by teachers and leaders learning together on the job about how to achieve their student learning goals. Chapter Six deals with leading teacher learning and development (Dimension Four). The two powerful ideas discussed in this chapter are collective responsibility for student learning and effective professional development. The latter discussion introduces readers to the evidence about the types of professional development that are more and less likely to make an impact on the students of the participating teachers. Just as for research on leadership, the ruler I use to judge the effectiveness of teacher professional learning or development is its impact on students.

The fifth dimension of student-centered leadership provides a foundation for all the rest. Student-centered leadership ensures an orderly and safe environment for staff and students. Teachers feel respected, students feel their teachers care about them and their learning, and school and classroom routines protect instructional time. The big ideas discussed in Chapter Seven are student engagement and two features of school organization that are strongly predictive of engagement—students' perceptions of safety and parent-school ties.

All research evidence is partial and subject to change as new evidence emerges. One obvious gap in Figure 1.1 is any reference to leaders' involvement with their various communities. The reason for this gap is not that this type of leadership is unimportant but that the research that contributed to Figure 1.1 included no measures of how leaders engaged their communities in the work of educating children. Without such measures we could not calculate the effects of this leadership dimension on student outcomes. Even though this type of information is missing, there is other evidence about the importance of trust between a school and its communities and about what leaders can do to build trust (Bryk & Schneider, 2002). That is why I have made many references to the work of engaging the community throughout this book, especially in the discussions of trust building in Chapter Two and of creating a safe and orderly environment in Chapter Seven.

The big message from the research on how leaders make an educational difference can be summed up as follows:

The more leaders focus their relationships, their work, and their learning on the core business of teaching and learning, the greater will be their influence on student outcomes.

At one of the first professional conferences where I presented these findings, I was asked if the five dimensions would be a good framework for evaluating principals. I replied that I would prefer they were used to evaluate the strength of leadership across the school or in particular departments or units. The scope of the work is too great and the expertise required too broad to reasonably expect a single leader to demonstrate high or even moderate levels of competence in all five dimensions.

Individual leaders may wish to get feedback on how strong they are in leading each area, but such developmental purposes are very different from holding individual leaders accountable on all five dimensions. Such accountabilities reinforce unrealistic conceptions of heroic leadership and deny the reality of distributed leadership in schools (Spillane, 2006). A more useful exercise is to involve the whole senior leadership team in a discussion of the emphasis currently given to each of these dimensions. One leadership team I have worked with reallocated leadership responsibilities to ensure that at least one team member had oversight of each of the dimensions. Other teams have independently rated the strength of school leadership on each dimension and then discussed their reasons for their various ratings.

Another question I am often asked is, "What has happened to relationships?" It is a good question because most theories of effective leadership make specific mention of relationship skills. My answer is that because relationships are central to success on *all* the dimensions, they are included not as a separate dimension but as one of three capabilities that informs them all. Effective educational leadership is not about getting the relationships right and then tackling the difficult work challenges. It is about doing both simultaneously so that relationships are strengthened through doing the hard, collective work of improving teaching and learning.

The "How" of Student-Centered Leadership: Three Capabilities

Student-centered leadership is about knowing *what* to do and *how* to do it. Although the five dimensions tell leaders *what* to focus on to make a bigger impact on students, they say little about the knowledge, skills, and dispositions needed to make the dimensions work in a particular school context. The knowledge and skills needed to engage confidently in these five dimensions are described in three broad leadership capabilities (see Figure 1.2).

First, student-centered leadership involves applying relevant knowledge to one's leadership practice. Although the depth of knowledge required for student-centered leadership is often

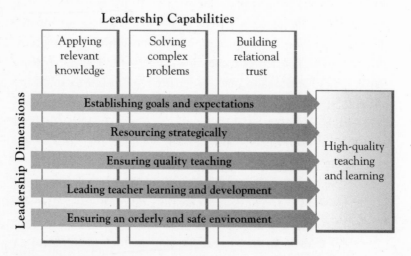

Leadership Capabilities

| Applying relevant knowledge | Solving complex problems | Building relational trust |

Leadership Dimensions

Establishing goals and expectations

Resourcing strategically

Ensuring quality teaching

Leading teacher learning and development

Ensuring an orderly and safe environment

High-quality teaching and learning

Figure 1.2   Five Dimensions Supported by Three Leadership Capabilities

underestimated, this capability is not about being highly qualified or getting high grades in courses about teaching and learning. Rather, it is about using knowledge about effective teaching, teacher learning, and school organization to make high-quality administrative decisions. In order to develop this capability, leaders need multiple opportunities to deepen their knowledge *and* consider its implications for administrative processes, such as teacher evaluation, student grouping, and curriculum choices.

The second capability required for student-centered leadership is skill in solving complex problems. If a high school leader wants to improve academic goal setting in subject departments, there is much more involved than learning about goal setting. In addition, the leader must be able to discern and overcome the challenges involved in implementing new goal-setting procedures in his or her particular context. Discerning what these challenges are and crafting solutions that adequately address them are the processes of problem solving. The account of problem solving that I provide in Chapter Two provides a model for good problem solving and uses research on leaders' problem solving to illustrate more and less skillful problem-solving processes.

The third capability involves building the type of trust that is essential for doing the hard work of improving teaching and learning. Leaders might understand the theory of student-centered leadership, but if they cannot develop trust among leaders, teachers, parents, and students they will have great difficulty practicing it. We know, for example, that many leaders have difficulty discussing their concerns about a teacher's classroom practice. In Chapter Two, I provide a detailed account of how to have such conversations in ways that both build trust and address the difficult issues. The values and skills involved in building trust provide an ethical foundation for all five leadership dimensions.

Student-centered leadership involves a skillful integration of the "what" and the "how" of leadership. Because I intend to demonstrate this integration in each of the five chapters devoted to a leadership dimension (Chapters Three through Seven), I introduce the three capabilities in Chapter Two so that readers will have some background principles before these are encountered in the discussion of each dimension. As depicted in Figure 1.2, the three capabilities are relevant to all five leadership dimensions.

Striking a Balance

Discussions of leadership can easily become extreme. Those who exaggerate its influence and importance attribute more influence, power, and energy to leaders than is either reasonable or realistic. Those who reject such heroic conceptions of leadership sometimes go to the opposite extreme, seeing school leaders as having little leverage over the most important determinants of student achievement. The truth no doubt lies somewhere in between. What is important to me in this book is to avoid both extremes by recognizing the challenges of the contexts in which leaders work while seeking to expand their influence over the learning of the students for whom they are responsible. The new research on which this book is based is a resource for doing just that. My hope is that it inspires leaders to experiment with changing how they lead and see if those changes, however small, expand their influence in ways that improve teaching and learning in their school.

Summary

The ruler I use in this book to judge the effectiveness of leadership is impact on the learning of those students for whom the leader is responsible. This ruler is justified by new research that shows that leaders can have a considerable effect on the social and academic achievement of their students. In schools where students achieve at higher-than-expected levels, leaders are much more focused on the improvement of teaching and learning than in similar schools where students perform at lower-than-expected levels. My analysis of this research identified five leadership dimensions that contribute to this focus: establishing goals and expectations, resourcing strategically, ensuring quality teaching, leading teacher learning and development, and ensuring an orderly and safe environment. In the following chapters I explain how each of these leadership dimensions works and provide rich examples of their use. I also introduce three leadership capabilities that leaders need in order to engage successfully in these five dimensions of student-centered leadership.

2

Three Capabilities for Student-Centered Leadership

What capabilities do school leaders need to be effective? Judging from the standards used to evaluate leaders in many education systems, the answer can include dozens of different qualities (Louden & Wildy, 1999; Reeves, 2009). Such lists present unrealistic and unattainable expectations for effective school leadership. They reinforce the heroic concept of leadership by implying that only a chosen few can succeed in a job that requires super human energy, high intelligence, strategic brilliance, and outstanding relationship skills. Yet people succeed in the job who do not demonstrate all these skills, or at least do so to far more modest levels than is implied by many such lists (Mintzberg, 2009).

The three leadership capabilities that I describe in this chapter were determined by asking, "What capabilities do leaders require to use the five dimensions of student-centered leadership in their own contexts?" On the basis of logical analysis and a modest amount of research literature, I propose the three capabilities introduced in Chapter One: applying relevant knowledge, solving complex problems, and building relational trust. Much more is known about effective leadership practices than about the capabilities required to enact them (Smylie & Bennett, 2005). Nevertheless, there are some seminal research studies that I have used extensively to identify and describe the leadership capabilities that support the five leadership dimensions described in this book.

Lists of leadership capabilities—even short ones—are not helpful if they are not enriched by discussion of the theory that explains how they work. That is why I include underlying principles, detailed illustrations, and practical guidance in my discussion of the three capabilities. Each capability is relevant to all five dimensions. Effective goal setting, for example, requires knowledgeable decision making about what goals to set and how to set them. Problem-solving skills are required to address the unique practical, interpersonal, and technical challenges to goal setting that arise in any given context. Finally, capability in building relational trust is essential to gaining staff agreement with and commitment to the goal-setting process and to the particular goals being set.

Even with only three broad capabilities, I risk falling into the heroic leadership trap if I imply that a single leader can or should reach a very high standard on all three. It is unrealistic to argue, for example, that high school principals require in-depth knowledge of multiple subject areas in order to be effective instructional leaders. I think it helps to make a distinction between the minimal levels of the capabilities that might be required by *every* educational leader and the desirability of strong *collective* capability across all three areas.

In order to avoid the perception of incompetence, a minimum standard on each of the three capabilities is desirable for any teacher in a leadership role. The head of department, the year-level leader, the literacy leader, and each member of the senior leadership team need sufficient knowledge and problem-solving and relationship skills, relevant to their area of responsibility, to demonstrate competence in their role. Beyond this minimal level, the goal should be to develop and recruit expertise in these three capabilities across the entire school leadership, recognizing the necessity for specialization, for sharing of expertise, and for learning opportunities that are tailored to each leader's particular responsibilities. The three capabilities serve as an ongoing agenda for leadership development.

Applying Relevant Knowledge

Student-centered leadership requires direct involvement with teachers in the business of improving teaching and learning.

But what do leaders need to know in order to get productively involved? In brief, they need to have access to up-to-date, evidence-based knowledge of how students learn and of how teaching promotes that learning in diverse classroom contexts. And they need to apply this knowledge when making decisions about, for example, teacher evaluation, resource selection, student grouping, and reporting to parents. As noted by Spillane and Seashore Louis (2002), "Without an understanding of the knowledge necessary for teachers to teach well—content knowledge, general pedagogical knowledge, content specific pedagogical knowledge, curricular knowledge, and knowledge of learners—school leaders will be unable to perform essential school improvement functions such as monitoring instruction and supporting teacher development" (p. 97). In short, there are two aspects to this capability: having relevant knowledge and applying it to the leadership practice in question.

Most school leaders sincerely believe that they make decisions that are in the best interest of students. But it is hard for them to test the validity of their belief without awareness of what they are assuming to be true and the ability to evaluate their assumptions against up-to-date evidence. My main purpose in this section is to explain how leaders' educational understandings shape their administrative practice and, therefore, how important it is to test the quality and administrative implications of those understandings.

Most of the examples I use come from a research and development program designed to improve the teaching of mathematics in the United States (Nelson & Sassi, 2005; Stein & Nelson, 2003). Part of the program involved a series of workshops for the principals of the participating elementary and high schools so they could learn how to support their teachers in making the shift from an emphasis on teaching computational fluency through drills and work sheets to teaching for mathematical reasoning and understanding. This required teachers to learn a more constructivist pedagogy in which they probed and challenged students' reasoning through various sorts of inquiry and through explicit comparison between different problem-solving strategies. Principals, in turn, needed to know enough about the new constructivist approach to ensure that their management of instruction was appropriately aligned to the new approach. Although the workshop involved principals, the examples are applicable to the work of any leader with responsibility for classroom observation and feedback to teachers.

Applying Relevant Knowledge to Decisions About Classroom Observation

If principals were to provide appropriate support for their teachers, they needed to know enough about the constructivist approach to math teaching to ensure that such procedures as classroom observation and feedback to teachers were appropriately aligned to the new approach. Table 2.1 shows how the principals' knowledge about effective teaching shaped the way they conducted classroom observations and gave feedback to their teachers. The first row in the table describes a principal who understood effective teaching from a behavioral rather than a constructivist point of view. Even though this principal was committed to a greater emphasis on teaching mathematical reasoning, he did not know enough about what such teaching looked like to give the teacher relevant feedback.

The second row in Table 2.1 describes a principal who understood more about what was involved in teaching for mathematical understanding but whose limited knowledge of such teaching meant he only attended to its surface features. By contrast, the third principal knew more about what the teaching of mathematical reasoning looked like and about the mathematical ideas involved in the lesson. As a consequence, she was able to observe and give feedback on the extent to which the teacher's questions were responsive to and extended the students' mathematical understandings.

In addition, this third principal became aware of a misalignment between the classroom observation procedures used in her school and the type of teaching required to increase mathematical

Table 2.1   The Relationship Between Three Principals' Pedagogical Understandings and Their Conduct of Classroom Observations

Principals' Pedagogical Understandings	Principals' Classroom Observations
1. Behaviorist pedagogy	Principal focuses on the observable features of the lesson and notes that the teacher 　　Begins with a short review 　　Gives clear and detailed instructions
2. Constructivist pedagogy Knowledge of surface features only	Principal focuses on the observable aspects of constructivist pedagogy and gives the teacher feedback on whether he 　　Asks sufficient open-ended questions 　　Checks for a variety of answers Does not observe or give feedback on the intellectual content of the lesson, such as the validity and sophistication of students' mathematical thinking and how the teacher is promoting that thinking
3. Constructivist pedagogy Knowledge of deeper features	Principal observes and evaluates how well the teacher is extending the students' mathematical reasoning. She records complete exchanges between the teacher and students to judge how well the teacher's questions connect with the students' reasoning. This judgment requires the principal to think through the relevant mathematical ideas.

understanding. She recognized that the existing observation checklist was encouraging unresponsive teaching because it did not evaluate how the teacher was responding to the thinking of the students. The principal then adopted a narrative form of recording so she could focus better on how the teacher's comments and questions were linked to the understanding and misunderstandings of the students. In short, the principal's knowledge of how to teach for mathematical understanding enabled her to recognize and correct a misalignment between her instructional goals and the administrative decisions she had previously made about how to evaluate the teaching of math.

⌐One could reasonably argue that it is unrealistic to expect principals to be as closely involved in classroom observation as the participants in this workshop. The jury is still out on how much detailed knowledge of effective teaching is needed by the principal, though the evidence I discuss in Chapter Six certainly suggests that principals who learn alongside their teachers tend to be found in high-performing schools. Whatever a principal's particular circumstances, the lesson I take from this example is that the principal needs sufficient knowledge to recognize and correct misalignments between administrative procedures and instructional purposes or to ensure that those responsible for the relevant administrative procedures are able to do so. ⌐

Applying Relevant Knowledge to Decisions About Curriculum Selection and Student Grouping

Nelson and Sassi (2005) discuss several other ways in which shifts in leaders' knowledge about teaching and learning change administrative practice. As one principal learned more about mathematics and math instruction, he changed the process of textbook selection from one dominated by pragmatic considerations (cost, content coverage, usability by teachers, attractiveness to students) to one in which the primary consideration was "What kinds of mathematical thinkers are produced by this text?" The mathematical and pedagogical content knowledge of the principal enabled him to (1) formulate the problem as a mathematical one as well as an administrative one, (2) write a series of questions that guided the selection committee to consider the type of mathematics being taught by the alternative texts, and (3) notice when the committee was straying into practical rather than mathematical considerations.

An elementary school principal used his knowledge of mathematics, of math teaching, and of teacher learning to structure a series of discussions about the grouping of students in math. He wanted teachers to consider the teaching implications of different types of grouping rather than make the decision in terms of the type of abstract principles enshrined in an equity policy. The two activities he designed enabled his teachers to study a real case of math teaching in heterogeneous groups and to experience heterogeneous grouping themselves as they worked together to solve a mathematics problem. One of the key ideas the principal wanted to convey to teachers was that diverse students in heterogeneous classes don't simply know more or less than each other—they approach mathematics in different ways, just as the teachers had done when solving their mathematics problem.

The two activities changed the way teachers thought about student grouping in mathematics. Homogeneous grouping was no longer an "obvious" solution to the problem of students working at different rates. Teachers now realized that heterogeneous grouping gave children more experience of different ways of solving the same problem and that this experience deepened their mathematical understanding.

The principal had used his knowledge of math teaching and learning to transform an administrative decision into an opportunity for teacher professional learning. One of the recurring themes of this book is that of alignment between administrative processes and instructional purposes. These examples show how detailed knowledge about the effective teaching of particular subjects enables leaders to align administrative procedures with important instructional objectives.

Solving Complex Problems

Although having good ideas is important for student-centered leadership, it is even more important that leaders can put them into practice. Ideas about how to develop student leadership, increase parent involvement, or create better assessment practices don't get any traction unless leaders can make them work in their particular context. Figuring out how to do that requires problem-solving skills.

As Ben Levin (2008) puts it in his book on leading change, "One of the challenges in education, as in other policy fields, is that the pizzazz is around having the seemingly new idea, whereas the real work is in making it happen. While innovations tend to get the profile, the slog work of implementation is what makes the difference in the end, and this work gets much less attention in the literature on education change" (pp. 5–6).

What is needed for implementation success, in addition to good ideas, is the ability to satisfy the conditions that need to be met if the idea is to work. Identifying and satisfying those conditions is the process of problem solving. A good way to identify these conditions is to discuss the idea with those who will be responsible for its implementation. Their reactions will tell you some of the conditions that they think need to be met by any acceptable solution.

Imagine a leader who wants teachers to report from a common assessment framework in a particular subject. She introduces the idea at a staff meeting and learns from the ensuing discussion that the five conditions in Table 2.2 are important to her teachers.

In summary, the wish list for the new assessment is that, as far as possible, it meets the needs of classroom teachers and external stakeholders, is readily communicated and interpreted, incorporates procedures that protect individual teachers, employs user-friendly technology, and does not add to the total student assessment burden! It is obvious that there is considerable tension among these various conditions. Indeed, some would argue that they are so much in conflict that it will be impossible to find a solution that satisfies all of them. For example, achievement data that satisfy external accountability requirements may tell teachers that improvement is needed but provide little useful diagnostic

Table 2.2   A Problem-Solving Skill: Identifying Solution Requirements

Staff Comments	Implied Solution Requirements
"We are required to inform the board of the assessment results."	Accountability to external stakeholders
"Parents could misinterpret the results."	Accuracy of interpretation
"It must be useful for my teaching."	Usefulness to classroom teachers
"In this political climate the information will be used to punish teachers."	Need to protect teachers from misuse of information
"I think we overassess students already."	New assessments must not add to total assessment burden
"The software needs to be easier to use."	Efficient technology

information. If more detailed diagnostic data are collected, the requirement to assist classroom teachers will be better satisfied but the technical burden of efficiently managing and collating the information may become too great (Sharkey & Murnane, 2006).

Creating a Satisfactory Solution

There is nothing unusual about this example. Tension among solution requirements is precisely what makes so many educational problems appear intractable and why none of them are ever *finally* solved. How then do leaders move from identifying solution requirements to finding a possible solution? The goal is to create a solution that as far as possible satisfies all the requirements that survive critical scrutiny. Critical scrutiny involves checking the validity or reasonableness of the proposed requirements. For example, the claim that "we overassess students already" can be scrutinized by asking about the basis of the claim (what subjects or year levels are seen as overassessed; what is the current assessment calendar for those students) and checking the extent to which others see the amount of assessment as excessive. If the claim of overassessment survives such scrutiny, then the proposed requirement that any new assessment not add to the total assessment burden must remain on the list of solution requirements. The inevitable implication is that any new assessment must replace an existing one.

Because there is so much tension among the various solution requirements, some will have to be given more weight than others, and it is likely that none will be fully satisfied. There are both attitudinal and cognitive challenges involved. The attitudinal challenge involves willingness to embrace *all* reasonable solution requirements and to craft solutions that give them appropriate weight rather than privilege one or two favored requirements. Leaders can encourage all participants to take responsibility for the *whole* problem by keeping the list of requirements in front of everyone and insisting that suggested solutions are evaluated against *all* of them.

Part of the cognitive challenge is to understand the solution requirements and their interdependence at the level of underlying principles rather than surface features. For example, one strategy for protecting teachers from misuse of assessment information might be to limit what is provided to outsiders. Although this strategy might appear satisfactory, it violates the principles of accuracy and openness that underlie the requirement for accountability and accuracy of interpretation. Rather than withholding information, a more principled and integrative approach might be to look for ways of protecting teachers by educating the audience about possible misinterpretations and inviting dialogue about the meaning of the assessment data. The deeper one's knowledge of the solution requirements, the more possibilities open up about how they may be integrated. Experts in their field are skilled problem solvers because their deep conceptual understandings enable them to see relationships among the various elements of the problem (Voss, 1989).

In my earlier writing on problem solving, I summarized the attitudinal and cognitive skills involved as follows:

Competing [solution requirements] are fulfilled, not by crass compromise or trade-offs between them, but by understanding their underlying principles and values so that more possibilities are revealed about how they may be satisfied. Inseparable from this knowledge is an attitude of <u>commitment to the whole prob-</u>lem, which motivates problem solvers to search for solutions that as far as possible satisfy [all the requirements] rather than maximize those they initially favored. Such integrative contributions are more likely to be made by those who are skilled at recognizing and creating common ground than by those who more readily perceive conflict and opposition. [Robinson, 2001, p. 98]

The goal is to find a solution that sufficiently satisfies the important requirements rather than maximizing one or two. Oppositional and binary thinking, for example, that assessment can never serve both formative and summative purposes, is particularly unhelpful when trying to integrate competing solution requirements.

Educational leaders are constantly tackling tasks that are replete with tensions, competing requirements, paradoxes, and inconsistencies. The approach to problem solving I have outlined here enables leaders to embrace those tensions, make them public, and seek principled ways of integrating them. The result will be a solution that is good enough to make a start on implementing the idea and to then see what happens. Inevitably, the problem will be revisited when more is known and the solution requirements change.

Leading the Problem-Solving Process

In education, <u>problem solving is not a solitary process.</u> It typically takes place in meetings so that the affected parties can contribute their ideas and shape the solution. Considerable insight into how to lead such meetings can be gained from a series of studies conducted by Ken Leithwood and his colleagues at the Ontario Institute for Studies in Education. In one study, they discovered important differences between how a group of expert and typical principals led a staff discussion of a problem that had to be solved in their school (Leithwood & Steinbach, 1995). The main findings of this study are reported in Table 2.3. They are based on analyses of principal interviews and of the meetings themselves.

What Leithwood calls *problem formulation* is akin to deciding the solution requirements—those conditions that have to be satisfied if a solution is to be workable and acceptable in *this* school. The expert principals were more open to alternative formulations of the problem because they tested their own assumptions about the problem and sought out the interpretations of others. Rather than treating problems in isolation, they linked the problem to wider school goals and to important values. This is an important skill because problems in schools are often tightly interconnected, and if this is not recognized, single problems can be solved in ways that make it harder to solve other problems for which the leadership team is responsible.

When it comes to the meeting process itself, the expert principals were more active in their facilitation of staff discussion and more concerned about reaching a genuinely shared solution. Their openness about their own views was motivated by a desire for feedback rather than a desire to win staff over to their preconceived solution.

In summary, capability in collective problem solving is essential for getting things done in schools. It involves formulating a problem by identifying the conditions that a solution needs to satisfy and creating an integrative solution that, as far as possible, meets those conditions. Expert leadership of collective problem-solving models requires ownership of the whole problem, disclosure of one's own view while remaining open to alternatives, and attention to the consequences of proposed solutions for wider school values and purposes.

Table 2.3   Principals' Problem Solving: A Comparison of Expert and Typical Principals

Expert Principals Are More Likely to . . .	Typical Principals Are More Likely to . . .
Problem Formulation	
1. Explicitly check own assumptions about problem	Assume others share their assumptions
2. Actively seek the interpretations of others	Not seek others' interpretations
3. Relate the problem to the wider mission of the school	Treat the problem in isolation from other problems and goals
4. Give a clear statement of their own interpretation of the problem, with reasons	Have difficulty explaining their view to staff
5. Develop goals that are widely shared	Focus on meeting own goals
6. Make value statements, especially those concerned with participation	Make fewer value statements
7. Anticipate obstacles and how they could be overcome	Anticipate fewer obstacles and see them as major impediments
Problem-Solving Process	
1. Carefully plan a collaborative problem-solving process	Do less planning of the process
2. Openly disclose own view without foreclosing or restraining other views	Not disclose own view or disclose in a controlling manner
3. Overtly manage meeting process, for example, summarizing and synthesizing staff views	Do less active meeting management
4. Experience and express little or no negative emotion and frustration	Experience unexpressed negative emotion and frustration

Building Relational Trust

I signaled in Chapter One that all five dimensions of student-centered leadership involve relationship skills. In this book I describe these skills as building trust because there is compelling evidence that the level of trust among the members of a school community makes an important difference to the way they work together and to the social and academic progress of students (Bryk & Schneider, 2002; Tschannen-Moran & Hoy, 2000). In schools with higher levels of trust, teachers experience a stronger sense of professional community and are more willing to innovate and take risks. In addition, students in high-trust schools make more academic and social progress than students in otherwise similar low-trust schools (see Figure 2.1).

The Determinants of Trust

School leaders build trust by modeling and expecting the four qualities on which it is based (Bryk & Schneider, 2002). The most

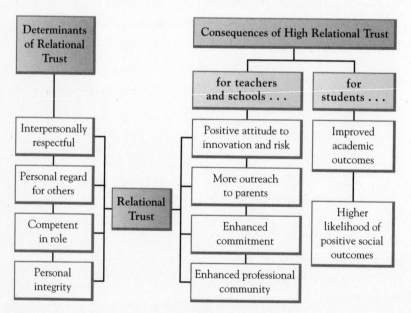

Figure 2.1   How Relational Trust Works in Schools

basic of these qualities is respect, which is demonstrated primarily by valuing the ideas of other people. Parents respect teachers who listen carefully to their concerns about what is happening to their children; teachers respect leaders who listen and are open to influence (see left-hand boxes of Figure 2.1).

The second determinant of trustworthiness is personal regard. Leaders earn trust by caring about the personal and professional lives of their staff. For example, meeting with a teacher for career planning and professional development purposes is likely to build trust because it signals that the leader cares. The knowledge that others care reduces one's sense of vulnerability, increases social affiliation, and invites reciprocal regard. Teachers need personal expressions of support as much as anyone else.

Competence is the third criterion on which discernments of trust are based. When people are reliant on others to succeed in the work of educating children, they care about their competence. In education it is often easier to discern incompetence than high competence because signs of incompetence are more public and less ambiguous. For example, teachers and parents are quick to make negative judgments about principal incompetence when buildings are not orderly and safe or when individuals interact in a disrespectful manner (Bryk & Schneider, 2002).

Judgments of leaders' competence are often based on how they deal with perceived incompetence in the staff for whom they are responsible. Allowed to persist, gross incompetence is highly corrosive to trust and undermines collective effort. Leaders who are conflict avoiders or conflict escalators are unlikely to deal with competence issues in a timely and effective manner. Because school improvement requires sustained collective effort, teachers may reduce their commitment if they judge that their leaders cannot deal with those who wittingly or unwittingly undermine the group's effort.

The fourth determinant of trust is integrity. Teachers make judgments about whether their leaders walk the talk, keep their word, and resolve difficult conflicts in a principled and even-handed manner. Bryk and Schneider (2002) write that "integrity demands resolutions that reaffirm the primary principles of the institution. In the context of schooling, when all is said and done, actions must be understood as advancing the best interests of children" (p. 26).

Building Trust While Tackling Tough Issues

Building trust requires leaders to deal effectively with perceived breaches of trust, including perceived poor performance, disciplinary matters, and failure to keep agreements. Yet it is precisely these situations that leaders struggle to deal with effectively. Leaders may want to address performance issues yet feel caught in a dilemma between addressing the issue and taking care of relationships (Cardno, 2007). Any issue that triggers this dilemma is a "tough" issue.

In a classic study of how administrators deal with teacher incompetence, Bridges (1986) found that the initial typical response to the dilemma was to tolerate, protect, and work around the issue. This was followed by a variety of treading-softly strategies in which the issues were understated or distorted. When this proved ineffective and administrators came under pressure to take more decisive action, they typically moved into a more direct "salvage" phase.

> During the salvage stage administrators abandon the practices of the earlier period. They no longer sprinkle their observation reports with glowing generalities. They no longer cloak their criticisms in the guise of constructive suggestions. They no longer inflate the evaluations of the incompetent teacher. Straight talk replaces double-talk. Teachers who have perhaps experienced years of double-talk and ceremonial congratulation predictably react defensively to this "out-of-the-blue" negative feedback. [pp. 48–49]

More recent evidence suggests that this pattern may have changed little. Both teachers and administrators believe that the number of teachers receiving unsatisfactory evaluations is far fewer than the number of unsatisfactory teachers (Pajak & Arrington, 2004).

The improvement of teaching and learning requires leaders at all levels to address concerns they have about the performance of staff for whom they are responsible. Such conversations can be difficult because they have the potential to threaten relationships. In the face of such threats, leaders often experience a dilemma between dealing with the task or problem and protection of their relationships. These dilemmas are not inevitable. They are the result of the type of thinking portrayed in Figure 2.2.

The dilemma between concern for the person and concern for the task is irresolvable under both possible strategies because the leader is not open to the views of the teacher. Having made up her mind that the program is terrible, there is no room for developing a shared understanding of the program. In the soft-sell strategy, the leader discourages debate by failing to disclose and check her

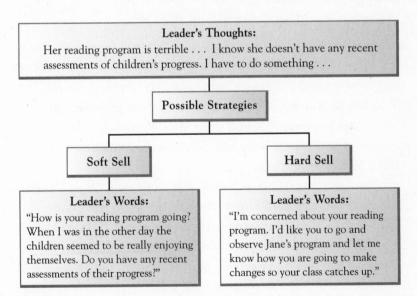

Figure 2.2   Two Ineffective Strategies for Dealing with Performance Problems

evaluation of the reading program. In the hard-sell strategy, the leader discourages debate by disclosing her views, assuming their truth, and then issuing instructions.

When leaders seek to impose their views rather than invite debate, they face the dilemma of how to do so without creating negative emotional reactions. The key to resolving this dilemma is not to hide one's own views in the hope that the other party will express what the leader is reluctant to disclose. This soft-sell strategy is just as closed minded as the more hard-sell strategy because the goal is still to win acceptance of one's views without being open to learning about their validity. In addition, leaders who convey their messages in such a soft-sell way risk not having them heard at all (Yariv, 2009). The key to resolving the dilemma is to change the thinking that leads the principal to assume rather than check the validity of her views. This means using what I call an open-to-learning rather than a closed-to-learning approach.

From Closed-to-Learning Conversations (CLCs) to Open-to-Learning Conversations (OLCs)

I turn now to the theory and practice that will help change the thinking that leads people to feel torn between maintaining relationships and dealing with the issue. The theory I am drawing on is based on that of Chris Argyris, a Harvard professor who has done extensive empirical and intervention research on the interpersonal effectiveness of leaders in on-the-job situations (Argyris, 1991, 1993).

The three interpersonal values that guide an OLC are widely endorsed but very hard to put into practice in difficult conversations such as those involving performance issues. The first value that guides a leader in an OLC is the pursuit of valid information. By "information" I mean thoughts, opinions, inferences, and feelings—anything that affects the views of the participants in the conversation. The validity value is especially critical for school leaders because their decisions have important implications for others' lives. Leaders have an ethical obligation, therefore, to make decisions based on high-quality information. Some of the key strategies associated with this value are disclosing your views and the reasoning behind them, seeking feedback from others, and treating your own views as hypotheses rather than as taken-for-granted truths.

The second value of respect means that others are treated as well intentioned, as having reasons for their actions, and as having the right to make informed choices. Respect for others involves listening deeply, especially when others disagree, and treating others as capable of learning and of contributing to one's own learning. Validity and respect are interdependent. Without respect, leaders will not be able to build the relational trust needed to get good feedback about their thinking.

The third value involves increasing the internal rather than external commitment of teachers to decisions. This is done through transparent and shared processes such as those discussed in the previous section on leading problem solving. When teachers have had the opportunity to exercise influence over the leadership, and when leaders, in turn, have been frank about their views and the limits of staff discretion, teachers are more likely to be committed to decisions and to the efforts required to implement them.

With this brief introduction to OLCs, I now return to the earlier example in Figure 2.2 of the dilemma between tackling a performance issue and maintaining the relationship. The leader can avoid an intractable dilemma by reframing her thinking about the reading program (see Table 2.4). She is still concerned about what she has seen, but rather than "sell" her view to the teacher she discloses it without expecting the teacher to share it or accept it. The purpose is not to win her over but to invite her into a conversation about the validity of both parties' views.

This third approach substantially reduces the dilemma because the concern is disclosed in a way that neither prejudges the situation nor protects the staff member from the possibility that

Table 2.4   An Open-to-Learning Approach to Communicating Performance Concerns

Leader's Thoughts	Leader's Words	Analysis
When I came into the class I was shocked to see the book levels being used. I suspect the students are well behind where they should be. I must talk to Joanne about how to check this.	*"When I came into your class the other day I got the impression from the book levels being used that many of your students were well behind where I would expect them to be. So I thought I should tell you that and check it against your understanding of their current and expected levels."*	The leader's concerns are disclosed. The grounds for the concern are disclosed. The leader indicates the concern needs to be checked rather than assumed to be valid.

change might be needed. Provided that the principal continues to disclose, check, listen, and co-construct the evaluation of the program and any changes to it, the result should be a teacher who feels challenged yet respected. The leader's thinking does not create an impossible choice between either tackling the educational issue or damaging the relationship.

The Key Components of an Open-to-Learning Conversation

There are no rules or step-by-step guides to open-to-learning conversations. This is because the shifts from closed to open-to-learning conversations are as much about changes in values and ways of thinking as they are about changes in communication skills. Hard and fast rules also do not work because good conversations are responsive to context and to the other person. Despite this, it is possible to identify some of the recurring components of open-to-learning conversations. Table 2.5 identifies some of them and shows how a leader might use them in conversations about a performance issue.

Table 2.5   Key Components of an Open-to-Learning Conversation About a Performance Issue

Key Components	What You Might Say
1. Describe your point of view without assuming its truth.	*"I don't know whether I'm right in this, but I was worried when I saw . . ."*
	"I need to tell you about a possible concern I have about . . ."
	"I think we may have different views . . ."
	"I realize this may not be how you see it, but I . . ."
	"I'm really disappointed in the art work because . . ."
2. Describe what your point of view is based on.	*"The reason why I was concerned is . . ."*
	"Yesterday when I was going past your classroom I heard . . ."
	"If I'm right, this is the third meeting you haven't been able to come to . . ."
	"I don't want parents demanding that their child be shifted. I want to work with you to address their concerns . . ."
3. Invite the other's point of view.	*[Pause and look at the other person.]*
	"What do you think?"
	"You haven't said much so far . . ."
	"Do you see it differently?"
	"I'm sure there is more to it than what I've said . . ."
	"This time I really want to understand more about your situation . . ."
	"How do you feel about the students' results?"
4. Paraphrase the other's point of view and check.	*"I got three important messages from [summarize]. Am I on the right track?"*
	"You're shaking your head; what have I missed?"

(Continued)

Table 2.5   (Continued)

Key Components	What You Might Say
5. Detect and check important assumptions.	*"What leads you to believe that the children aren't yet ready to read?"* *"What would be an example of that?"* *"What other possibilities are there?"* *"How would you know if your assumptions were wrong?"* *"What evidence do you have about the effectiveness of this math package?"*
6. Establish common ground.	*"We both agree this is unacceptable as it is . . ."* *"It sounds like we see the problem the same way."* *"We both want [summarize] but we have different ideas on how to get there."* *"We see the cause of the disruption differently, but we both want to do something about it."*
7. Make a plan to get what you both want.	*"How would you like to learn more about the new curriculum requirements?"* *"Okay—you will talk with your colleagues and let me know next week how they explain the results."*

The examples in Table 2.5 are my own compilation, but other versions are also worth exploring (Stone, Patton, & Heen, 2000). In my experience of leading workshops for school leaders on building relational trust, leaders can begin to interrupt their closed-to-learning patterns after two days of theoretical explanation, modeling, coaching, practice, and feedback using their own on-the-job performance issues. Skill in OLC is worth developing because it is critical to tackling the tough issues that I have highlighted in this section—particularly for concerns about performance. But OLC is more than a set of techniques to be trotted out in difficult conversations. The values of the model provide the ethical base for all leadership action and for building a culture of collaborative inquiry and learning throughout the school. Their application to all five leadership dimensions is explained and illustrated throughout the remainder of this book.

Summary

To put it in its simplest terms, student-centered leadership requires being knowledgeable about how to align administrative procedures to important learning outcomes, being skilled in using that knowledge to solve important school problems, and doing both of these things in ways that build relational trust in the school community.

Although I discussed each of these three capabilities separately, there are clear overlaps and interdependencies among them. For example, the capacity to solve problems is dependent on the depth and organization of leaders' relevant knowledge of their contexts and of the research evidence about how quality teaching supports student learning. Further, many of the skills associated with expert problem solving, such as actively seeking others' interpretations and openly disclosing personal views, are precisely the skills that build trust. Leadership is not about building trust so that the hard work of improvement can happen later. It is about tackling the work in ways that build trust through learning and making progress together.

3

Dimension One
Establishing Goals and Expectations

Schools are complex organizations with multiple competing agendas. Each agenda has its champions who argue for their preferred curriculum, teaching approach, or budget priority. Constantly changing external policy agendas contribute to the complexity. With each change of government, something else is added to the long list of school responsibilities, and only rarely is anything subtracted. Under these conditions, it is easy to see why schools can become fragmented and incoherent rather than united and purposeful.

One of the ways that leaders can reduce fragmentation and promote coherence is through the process of setting and communicating clear goals. By setting clear goals, leaders communicate the *relative* importance of these various agendas. Goal setting in education is not about deciding what is and is not important because a cogent argument can be made by someone for the importance of practically any current or proposed activity. Goal setting works because it forces decisions about *relative* importance— about what is more important in *this* context, at *this* time, than all the other important things.

Goal setting includes deciding what goals to set, gaining the commitment of those responsible for achieving them, and communicating them to all those with an interest in their achievement. The quality of goal setting cannot be separated from the quality of relationships. Leaders can set goals, but they will remain empty words unless they motivate those whose efforts are required to achieve them.

The Effect of Goal Setting on Student Outcomes

Goal setting is the first of five leadership dimensions whose effects on student learning and achievement were summarized in Figure 1.1. This dimension of leadership has, on average, a moderate impact on student outcomes. It works indirectly by focusing and coordinating the work of adults around promoting the learning and achievement of students. In schools where teachers report strong goal-setting activity by leaders, students will, on average, achieve significantly more than in otherwise similar schools. The leadership of higher-performing schools gives more emphasis than does its counterparts in lower-performing schools to communicating goals and expectations, informing the community of academic accomplishments, and recognizing academic achievement. In higher-performing schools teachers also report that there is more consensus about school goals.

These results are confirmed by several other reviews of the research evidence about how leaders make a difference to students. Ken Leithwood's review of the influence of leadership on school organization and student outcomes for the Department of Education and Skills in England includes "setting direction" as one of the practices of successful leaders (Leithwood, Harris, & Hopkins, 2008). A second comprehensive review of forty studies of principalship across all school types concluded that principals influence school academic performance by establishing an academic focus through clear shared goals (Hallinger & Heck, 1998). In schools that are strong on this leadership dimension, teachers are more likely to endorse survey items, such as "the principal makes student achievement the school's top goal" and "schoolwide objectives are the focal point of reading instruction in this school."

Despite this evidence about the importance of goal setting for increasing schoolwide student achievement, it is important to recognize the ways in which it can be misused, particularly when associated with imposed targets and punitive consequences.

My goal in this chapter is to explain how goal setting works in ways that enable leaders to avoid its misuse and take advantage of its considerable potential benefits for teachers and students.

How Goal Setting Works

Figure 3.1 provides a starting point for understanding how goal setting works (Latham & Locke, 2006). Three conditions need to be in place. People need to feel personally committed to the goal and believe they have the capacity to achieve it. The goal also needs to be specific so people can monitor their progress toward it. Given those three conditions, goal setting works by creating a discrepancy between the current situation and an attractive future. This discrepancy motivates people to focus their effort and attention on the activities required to reach the goal and to persist until they achieve it.

People achieve or learn more when goals are set under these conditions than if they are urged to "do their best" or to pursue vague goals. When people are committed to specific goals and believe they have the capacity to achieve them, goal setting can bring important psychological benefits. When teachers (and

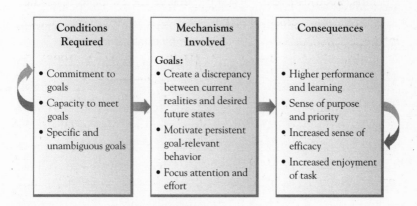

Conditions Required	Mechanisms Involved	Consequences
• Commitment to goals • Capacity to meet goals • Specific and unambiguous goals	**Goals:** • Create a discrepancy between current realities and desired future states • Motivate persistent goal-relevant behavior • Focus attention and effort	• Higher performance and learning • Sense of purpose and priority • Increased sense of efficacy • Increased enjoyment of task

Figure 3.1   How Goal Setting Works

leaders!) feel stressed by multiple conflicting priorities and work overload, goal setting helps them sleep at night because it forces explicit consideration of what has high priority, what has lower priority, and what must be let go altogether. The consequence should be an increased sense of purpose, personal efficacy, and job satisfaction.

Goals are often set with insufficient consideration of how to win the commitment and develop the capacity of those who are responsible for achieving them. It is all very fine to extol the virtues of goal setting but doing so without considering how to establish the conditions to make it work provides little practical help to school leaders. In the following three sections I explain more about how to establish these conditions and what to do when they cannot be met.

Gaining Goal Commitment

People commit to goals that they believe are important. Goals become important when people can see how they serve what they already value. Pursuit of the goal becomes attractive because it provides an opportunity for reducing the gap between the vision and the current reality. This means that two things are required for goal commitment. The goal needs to provide an opportunity to achieve what is valued, *and* people need to accept that the current situation falls sufficiently short of that vision to warrant pursuit of the goal.

A great deal has been written about the role of vision and values in educational leadership, and I have already acknowledged its importance in gaining goal commitment. But, as I warned at the outset of this chapter, there are also pitfalls to be avoided. Leaders who propose a new teaching practice, form of parent involvement, or budget allocation process need to connect their own values and passions for such changes with the values and passions of those who will implement them. This is a relational process, which is quite different from the ability of leaders to make inspirational speeches or write mission statements about what they value.

The vision must be collective rather than that of a single leader and it must emerge through discussion rather than be imposed (Fullan, 1992). In Chapter Two, I talked about how experts lead collaborative problem solving by expressing their own values and commitments and listening to those of others. Exactly the same principles apply to developing an attractive vision. Leadership does need to articulate, and at times demonstrate, alternative approaches and possibilities. But it also needs to listen to the passions of others and be a sensitive observer of what they care about.

Even when people appear to be endorsing similar value positions, it is important to explicitly check others' commitments. For example, New Zealand school leaders are learning that they cannot assume that goals about raising student achievement have the same motivational force in indigenous (Maori) communities that they have in the New Zealand European (Pakeha) community. Increased Maori student achievement has frequently meant loss of language and culture because young people have felt forced to choose between success in a Maori or a Pakeha world. Achievement goals for Maori students are only attractive to their community when explicitly linked to the value of educational success as a Maori—a value that explicitly recognizes the importance of integrating cultural and academic success.

A vision that does not make a difference to how a school operates is just empty words. A school that espouses "every child reaching his or her potential" but does not anchor this abstraction in specific goals is unlikely to achieve what it espouses. The vision talk must inform the goal-directed walk. In a study of principals of Australian high schools it was found that the stronger the principal's espousal of abstract vision statements the more negative the teachers' reactions (Barnett, McCormick, & Conners, 2001). The negative reactions of the teachers were due to a perceived discrepancy between the "talk" and the "walk" of their principals. Inspirational visions that stay at the level of words and symbols soon fail to inspire.

The second aspect of gaining goal commitment is acceptance of the gap between the goal and the existing state of affairs. Many leaders, including policy makers, focus only on the desirability of the goal and not on the difference between what they envisage and the present situation. They extol the virtues of a new innovation, but no one is quite sure why it is needed. Perhaps they believe that "moving forward," to use that dreadful cliché, requires them to focus on the future and avoid being "negative" about the present. This is a mistake because goal commitment requires people to understand how what they have now differs from what they truly want. If people don't perceive a discrepancy, or a problem that is worth acting on, they will not be convinced of the need for change and will not commit to the hard work required to achieve it. They may also believe that they are already doing most or all of what is being proposed. This is a common reaction to professional development that does not provide teachers with sufficient opportunities to study the difference between their current practice and the alternative that is being proposed by the professional development provider.

When I ask leaders why they avoid discussion of the difference been what they want and what they have got, their explanation is often couched in terms of maintaining relationships. They fear that discussion of the shortfalls of the present will be taken as criticism of their teachers and of themselves. This fear, plus a view of school public relations as requiring a stream of good news stories, means that many leaders have had little experience with what I call constructive problem talk. Such talk involves naming, describing, and analyzing problems in ways that reveal the possibilities for change. It is constructive because it contributes to a shared understanding of the current situation, avoids blame, and invites a collaborative approach to improvement. Constructive problem talk builds trust because people respect leadership that can own problems and take responsibility for solving them.

In his book describing the strategies used by ten U.S. school districts to turn around failing schools, Odden (2009) describes how one strategy they had in common was the setting of very ambitious goals. These districts set out to double student performance, and in many cases they achieved this goal. Communities encouraged school leaders to be ambitious after frank discussion of the poor levels of current achievement. Educators are often afraid to share such information for fear that it will lead to criticism of the school and withdrawal of students. Odden argues, however, that the process of public disclosure can produce just the opposite response—strong community encouragement to set very high goals.

These principles of how to gain goal commitment apply equally to goals that are set by school staff and those that are set for them. In the latter case, the challenge for school leaders is to frame these external goals as opportunities to achieve something that the school already values. Assuming some degrees of freedom, the implementation of the goal is tailored to serve the internal and the external agendas. In the words of Henry Mintzberg (2009), who rejects sharp distinctions between leaders and managers, "Effective managers, no matter where in the hierarchy and how seemingly constrained, grab whatever degrees of freedom they can get and run vigorously with them" (p. 216). This is exactly how some school leaders in the United States have responded to the adequate yearly progress (AYP) performance goals that are imposed on them as part of the federal No Child Left Behind legislation. Despite the ambitiousness of these goals, they have framed them as opportunities to pursue their own equity agendas (Rorrer & Skrla, 2005).

Checking Capacity to Achieve Goals

Goal setting works when people are committed to goals that they believe they have *the capacity to achieve*. Commitment and capacity are highly interdependent because people will not commit to goals that they believe they cannot achieve.

One of the traps in goal setting is to overestimate its motivational power and underestimate its requirement for relevant capacity. Capacity issues are likely to loom large in educational goal setting because the task of improvement is complex. Complexity arises from the numerous steps required to achieve the goal, uncertainty about the relationships between each step and the intended outcomes, and the large amount of information that needs to be taken into account. For such complex tasks, effort is not sufficient for goal achievement. Effective strategies are also required, and teachers who have failed to achieve the goal so far are likely to need considerable help in learning such strategies.

When the responsible system lacks the capacity to achieve a particular goal, leaders should initially set learning rather than performance goals. Performance goals are about the achievement of a specific outcome, such as increasing student enjoyment of school by a given percentage, raising the satisfaction level of staff, or completing a building project on time and on budget. It is assumed that those responsible have the skills and abilities needed to achieve the goal and that performance will be increased by motivating them to apply that knowledge to the specific task.

A learning goal, by contrast, focuses on the "discovery of the strategies, processes, or procedures to perform the task effectively" (Latham & Locke, 2007, p. 294). Attention is directed to learning how to do the task rather than achieving a specific outcome. The following example illustrates the distinction. Despite a district initiative to improve narrative writing, an evaluation shows that students are still achieving well below the expected level. It turns out that the professional development program taught teachers how to motivate writing (talking about key ideas, researching the topic, and teacher modeling of writing) but did not teach the structures and skills of narrative writing (for example, the structure of a story and of a paragraph, narrative sequence, and so on).

It makes no sense to set a new performance goal, such as 80 percent of students at a particular grade level will meet the standard in narrative writing by a certain date, when it is clear that neither the teachers nor the district advisors know how to reach the goal. The system has already established that despite attention, effort, and the investment of some resources, it lacks the capacity to achieve the goal.

What is needed are learning goals that require inquiry into how to teach narrative writing and to locate proven programs and expertise. Such goals create the space for learning how to do the work that goal achievement requires and prevent premature selection of ineffective strategies (Seijts & Latham, 2005). If leaders set challenging goals on complex tasks without considering teachers' capacity to achieve them, they are likely to raise counterproductive levels of anxiety and resentment, especially if those goals are accompanied by incentives and sanctions. They are also likely to create the very conditions under which teachers manipulate the targets rather than focus on the educational processes that the targets are intended to represent (Hargreaves & Fink, 2006).

There is something deeply unjust about holding people accountable for achieving performance targets when those who set them have little understanding of the tasks involved and even less understanding of the extent to which those who are required to achieve them have the requisite knowledge and skills. The same point that I made in the previous section on goal commitment applies here—understand and discuss the current reality before trying to change it through goal setting. This does not mean spending months on research, but it does mean doing sufficient inquiry to temper ambition with some plausible estimates of the current level of performance, of the amount and type of work required to lift that performance to proposed goal levels, and of the match between current capacity and the capacity required to bridge the gap. When leaders address capacity issues at an early stage, they learn whether to set learning or performance goals and build a culture in which learning to do the work rather than manipulating the indicators becomes the path to better performance.

Given a choice, teachers and leaders sometimes set easy goals because they do not trust the system to which they are accountable for goal performance. They fear they will be blamed or otherwise sanctioned for falling short of goal achievement and so they react defensively by setting goals that are well within their capacity to achieve. Leaders can reduce such defensiveness by discouraging trivial goals and modeling and rewarding learning from the setbacks and failures that are an inevitable part of the pursuit of more ambitious ones.

Setting Specific Goals

One of the most common pieces of advice about goal setting is the need for specificity. It is enshrined in the acronym about setting SMART goals—goals that are specific, measurable, achievable, realistic, and time bound. On the whole, goals are specific when they include criteria by which progress and achievement can be judged. SMART goals are often expressed as targets that describe the level of desired performance (for example, percentage increase in achievement) and the time by which it is to be achieved. In launching the Blair government's literacy initiative in England in 1997, the minister of education declared that within four years the percentage of children reading at the national standard for twelve-year-olds would rise from the current 55 percent to 80 percent (Levin, 2008).

At one level, setting SMART goals makes sense because people cannot regulate their performance if they are unclear about how to assess their progress. Take the goal set by a principal as part of his annual performance evaluation—to "improve relationships in the senior leadership team." This goal is vague because it does not provide clear criteria about what counts as improvement. Without such criteria, neither the principal nor his evaluator will be able to tell whether the relationships are improving and thus whether different strategies are required.

At another level, there are occasions when the call to set SMART goals is inappropriate. In order to set a SMART goal, you have to know quite a lot about how to achieve it. When goals involve new challenges, how can you possibly know if it is achievable, if it is realistic, and how long it will take you to achieve it (Seddon, 2008)? In the absence of such knowledge, it may be better to set a learning goal or a broader performance goal that expresses your shared commitments and helps keep you focused. Then as you learn more about how to achieve your goals, you can revisit them and make them more specific. It is this iterative learning and revising of targets that generates meaningful specificity.

How Many Goals?

A colleague and I recently completed a study of the goals experienced principals set as part of their annual performance evaluation. On average, they set six goals each, and fewer than 5 percent were learning goals. Although there are no hard and fast rules about an appropriate number of goals, there are several reasons why three or four would probably be better than six. Goals are set in areas of school life in which the intent is to improve on business as usual. This means old routines are disrupted, new ones are invented or adapted, and everyone has to learn how to embed the new routines into the daily work. At the same time, business as usual has to continue in every other area of school life. And that is a tall order in itself when schools are subject to so many unanticipated disruptions, distractions, and surprises (Levin, 2008). When natural disasters or student tragedies strike, health and safety take precedence over everything else. When the state department responds to a new report on the impending obesity and diabetes epidemic by requiring all elementary schools to introduce compulsory physical exercise for all students, new curriculum priorities must somehow be accommodated. These are the inevitable distractions from goal achievement.

Leaders may be tempted to set too many goals as a way of mitigating conflict or trying to gain wider commitment. In terms of the problem-solving principles introduced in Chapter Two, this constitutes an unsatisfactory solution to the problem of how to reconcile the requirement for commitment *and* goal achievement because too little weight has been placed on the latter. Too many goals defeat the purpose of giving clear messages about what has priority. A more integrative approach to these conflicting requirements could involve setting more overarching goals under which people can pursue subgoals that are explicitly aligned to the overarching goal. Another option is to develop a sequence of goals that are pursued when earlier ones are achieved.

Challenges to Goal Setting

Table 3.1 summarizes some of the challenges to goal setting that leaders are likely to encounter and provides strategies for a principled response to those challenges.

Table 3.1   Goal Setting: Common Challenges and How to Overcome Them

Challenges	Strategies
• People lack the skills and knowledge to achieve the goal.	• Set relevant learning rather than performance goals.
• Individuals' goals may be in conflict with each other.	• Set team or overarching goals.
• Failure to achieve goals is seen as a risk.	• Encourage and reward learning from mistakes.
• Accountability for goal attainment can produce biased and inaccurate reporting.	• Reward learning from mistakes, model and expect ethical practice, *and* consistently confront unethical practice.

- Successful goal attainment can reinforce old strategies that are inappropriate in a changing environment.
- Important outcomes that are not set as goals may be ignored.

- Invite robust critique and review of goals and strategies for reaching them.
- Set more inclusive goals. Monitor all critical outcomes while selecting a few for goal setting.

An additional challenge in achieving goals is developing the routines that enable teachers to integrate goal pursuit into their daily work. Without such routines, business as usual will drive out goal achievement. Here is how an elementary school teacher describes the importance of the routine that her leader developed to ensure that teachers met to review the data on their students' reading every five weeks. The regularity of the review meant that she and her colleagues kept a sharp focus on their goal to lift every student's reading level to the required standard.

Teacher: Well I keep saying the word focus. . . . If you don't have that focus, well then another five weeks goes by and things can crop up, like you can do some folk dancing and a marvelous unit on this and that. Now we know that every five weeks we are doing the [review], and you don't let reading go, you let other things go, but you don't let that go. . . . We used to think about getting through the day, keeping the room tidy, having a quiet class. At the end of the day, we would go home with a warm fuzzy feeling. "Oh, that was a good day. Maybe I will do some more of that tomorrow." I think the focus has come right back to "what have I done today, in reading today, who is moving and who isn't moving and why aren't they moving." That is what you are taking home in your head. [Timperley, 2005a, p. 409]

One of the lessons of goal setting is that you achieve what you focus on.

Reflective Questions About Dimension One Leadership

The following questions can be used to provide an informal assessment of the effectiveness of the leadership of goal setting in your school. You may wish to add questions to suit your own purposes and school context. If the questions are answered by teachers and leaders independently, then teachers' responses provide feedback to leaders about whether they evaluate goal setting in the same way. The information gained from such an informal survey can provide a starting point for a rich discussion about the effectiveness of the practices involved in this leadership dimension.

How effectively does [insert the principal, the subject head, the faculty head, or a particular leadership team, depending on who is the focus of the informal assessment] ensure that . . .

- There is agreement in this school, department, or team about the importance of the current learning goals?
- There is clear alignment between overarching school goals and the goals set by middle leaders for subjects and year levels?
- Teachers are clear about the learning goals for which they are responsible?
- Teachers feel personally committed to achieving the goals for which they are responsible?
- Teachers have the knowledge and skills they need to achieve the goals for which they are responsible?
- Teachers have the resources needed to achieve the goals for which they are responsible?

Summary

In this chapter I explained how leaders can enjoy the benefits of goal setting while avoiding its misuse. Setting specific goals increases performance when people are committed to the goal and believe they have the capacity to achieve it. When these conditions are in place, goal setting works because it focuses effort and attention and enables people to adjust their effort and their strategy in response to feedback about their level of progress.

I argued that leaders should not set challenging performance goals, especially when they are expressed as targets, if they do not know what is involved in achieving them. Without such knowledge, tight targets and associated accountability measures can be arbitrary and punitive, inviting gaming of the targets and driving out the learning and risk taking needed for the hard work of improvement. When the required capacity is insufficient, leaders should set learning rather than performance goals. The same principles apply—people should be committed to and have the capacity to tackle their learning goals.

Goals represent areas of school life in which the intent is to improve on business as usual. Because business as usual must continue in every other area, and there are the inevitable disruptions and crises, it makes sense to set no more than three or four main goals. The leadership of goal setting requires open-to-learning conversations that check and build commitment to goals, that model constructive problem talk, and that inquire at an early stage about capacity issues.

4

Dimension Two
Resourcing Strategically

Strategic resourcing is simple to explain and complicated to do. Leaders who take a strategic approach to resourcing ensure that money, time, and people are used in ways that reflect priority goals. These goals drive how they organize budgets, timetables, and staffing. If a school has committed to a goal of improving boys' love of reading, then that commitment should be reflected in decisions about the focus of teachers' professional development, the choice of appropriate texts and supplementary readers, and the criteria for hiring a new head of English language arts. Staffing, teaching resources, and teacher professional development are orchestrated in ways that increase the chance of achieving the goal.

The key focus of this chapter is not how to acquire additional resources but how to evaluate and reconfigure existing patterns of resource allocation. I pose questions and present research findings that might interrupt taken-for-granted assumptions about resource allocation. Questions that can encourage a fresh look at how money, time, and people are allocated include the following: "Are current patterns of expenditure aligned to priority learning goals? Does research evidence support our choice of instructional tools and resources? Are there more flexible ways of scheduling teacher and student time to meet the differing learning needs of students?"

Educators typically assume that additional money is the sine qua non of improvement. After all, the reasoning goes, if already overworked teachers are not meeting the needs of some students, then additional staff, programs, or both must be required.

This thinking is reinforced by the fact that reform initiatives are typically accompanied by new money—partly as an incentive for school involvement and partly in recognition of the extra effort that any change requires. But the evidence on the effects of additional resourcing is mixed at best. Take the case of per-pupil expenditure. Above a minimum threshold, there is little evidence that more money means better achievement. There is wide variation in per-pupil expenditure between comparable high-performing schools and a similarly wide variation in the per-pupil expenditure of low-performing schools (Miles & Frank, 2008). What matters is how the money is used.

A great deal of complexity has to be managed if alignment between priorities and resourcing is to be achieved. Managing that complexity requires a leadership team that has high levels of the three capabilities discussed in Chapter Two. First, leadership needs to make thoughtful and informed decisions about the type of staffing and instructional resources that are most likely to promote goal achievement. Because the majority of goals are about student achievement, this chapter summarizes pertinent evidence about the effectiveness of different types of staffing and instructional resources.

Second, capability in problem analysis and problem solving is required to critically evaluate current patterns of resource allocation and the assumptions on which they are based. An analytic orientation also ensures that new programs and initiatives serve core priorities and that those that detract are eliminated (Bryk, Sebring, Allensworth, Luppescu, & Easton, 2010). This chapter identifies problematic assumptions about resourcing, describes alternative approaches, and refers readers to practical guides about the reallocation of resources.

Third, managing the allocation and reallocation of resources requires a leadership team to have good relational skills to work through the human side of the process. Resource allocation and reallocation involve people's jobs, and courage is needed to face the inevitable emotional reactions to leaders who are determined and persistent in their pursuit of learning goals. In their book on strategic resourcing, Miles and Frank (2008) put it this way: "Any significant change in the use of resources means teacher and other staff jobs *will* be affected. Using school resources more effectively takes courage because it means setting priorities and being strong enough to say that some things are simply more important than others—even when these priorities demand ending a cherished program" (p. xi).

Persistence and a long time horizon are needed because prior patterns of resourcing cannot be changed overnight. There are also considerable constraints in the form of union contracts and district and state regulations and priorities about how time, teachers, and money can be allocated. In some large urban districts, for example, school leaders may have little control over either the recruitment or hiring process. Nevertheless, a leadership team that is knowledgeable about the research evidence and able to use it in open-to-learning conversations with district officials is likely to be more influential than teams that lack such knowledge and skills.

The Effect of Resourcing Strategically on Student Outcomes

Resourcing strategically is the second of five leadership dimensions whose effects on student achievement were summarized in Chapter One. The evidence for this dimension was derived from seven different studies of the relationship between leadership and student achievement. These studies included measures of leaders' involvement in recruiting staff, securing instructional resources, and making decisions about resource allocation (Andrews & Soder, 1987; Heck, Larsen, & Marcoulides, 1990). One study also asked teachers to report how knowledgeable their principal was about instructional resources (Bamburg & Andrews, 1991). When the results of these various measures were combined, the average effect of these leadership practices was 0.31, suggesting that this type of leadership has a small, indirect impact on student achievement.

The leadership measures that contributed to this dimension tell us more about leaders' involvement in resourcing than about whether it is strategic. They also tell us very little about the practical challenges of recruiting and allocating staff, instructional resources, and instructional time in ways that support the achievement of priority goals. When discussing those matters, I have drawn heavily on the work of Karen Miles and Stephen Frank (2008) and Allan Odden (Odden, 2009; Odden & Archibald, 2001). These books contain practical guides to strategic resource allocation and case studies of U.S. schools in which resource reallocation has been central to their improved performance.

Strategic Decisions About Staffing

The quality of teaching is the most powerful school-level influence on student achievement. Indeed, there is new evidence that teacher quality has cumulative effects. Students who experience consistently high-quality teaching will outperform initially similar students in both reading and math (Rivkin, Hanushek, & Kain, 2005). Conversely, students who experience below-average teaching over several years will struggle to catch up (Konstantopoulos & Chung, 2010). Leadership teams at both district and school levels can improve the quality of teaching through their approach to the recruitment, retention, and replacement of staff. Improving teaching through systematic teacher professional learning and development is also a critical leadership responsibility and is dealt with in Chapter Six.

Leaders often attribute difficulties in recruitment and retention to a shortage of qualified teachers. Although this explanation has some empirical support, the teacher labor market, in the United States at least, suffers more from a revolving door problem than from a shortage of supply (Ingersoll, 2001). Unless problems of retention are addressed, increased supply will only increase the traffic through the revolving door.

Although national and district employment policies and practices are important, research suggests that staff retention and recruitment are also responsive to school-based practices and policies (Ingersoll, 2001). While it is true that retention rates differ between teachers of different age and subject specialty, and between schools of different type and location, what goes on in the school has a considerable *additional* effect on staff retention. The more effective the support for new employees in areas of student discipline, curriculum, instructional method, and induction, the less turnover of teachers. Schools that give staff more influence over decisions about curriculum, teaching, and professional development are also likely to enjoy a lower turnover rate than comparable schools where teachers experience less inclusive instructional decision making. Finally, schools where teachers report fewer student discipline problems have less turnover than comparable schools with more problems of student discipline.

Richard Ingersoll's analysis is good news for school leaders because it means that they may have more influence over the causes of teacher turnover than they thought possible. Developing instructional support for staff, a more collegial environment, and better student discipline are central to the learning of teachers and students. The by-product of such improvements may also be a more committed and loyal staff. Because schools with high turnover also tend to have recruitment difficulties, these steps may also make the school more attractive to teacher applicants.

When it comes to recruitment, the same message applies— rather than assume a shortage of qualified teachers, it is more fruitful for school and district leaders to focus on the development of proactive and comprehensive recruitment strategies. Odden (2009) describes how three poorly performing urban school districts—New York, Boston, and Chicago—included such strategies in reforms that resulted in a doubling of student achievement and qualification levels. Their strategic staffing approach included partnerships with high-quality local teacher-education providers, which gave them access to a large pool of new teachers. Teachers were also actively recruited through such alternative providers as Teach for America, many of whom stayed longer than their initial contracts. Strong induction, mentoring, and incentives also improved recruitment and retention rates. Some districts also ran their own teacher- and principal-training programs to ensure that the preparation was tailored to district needs and that the participants were given high-quality, school-based mentoring.

Based on their extensive work with many different types of schools in the United States, Miles and Frank (2008) have drawn some important conclusions by comparing the hiring practices of average and high-performing schools. These authors are clear that although school leaders in some districts have limited discretion over staffing, systemic improvement at the district level should be based on careful study of what is needed at the school level. If district leaders learn from this bottom-up approach, they can reform district policies and procedures in ways that enable many more schools to achieve what has been done in these high-performing schools. The authors' comparison shows that high-performing schools are more likely to fill individual vacancies based on a long-term staffing plan that has been developed from an analysis of the match between student learning needs and current staff capability. Job descriptions and advertisements are tailored to particular positions and communicate clear expectations about the purpose, skills, and work schedule associated with the job. The selection process goes beyond an interview to include lesson demonstrations and discussion of the candidate's commitment to the learning goals and instructional framework relevant to the position.

A strategic approach to staffing also includes the reallocation of the resources being spent on consistently poor-performing staff. Natural justice and employment law require school leaders to clearly communicate their concerns about performance, to provide opportunities for improvement, and to follow a careful and documented process. Although such conversations are never easy, they are more likely to be conducted in a timely and effective manner if leaders bring the skills and values of an open-to-learning conversation to the discussion. When clear feedback and high-quality learning opportunities do not produce the desired improvement, leaders may need to terminate employment and recruit higher-quality replacement staff.

The Allocation and Impact of Teacher Aides

In many educational systems there has been a considerable expansion of in-class teaching assistants, variously known as teacher aides (TAs), teaching assistants, or learning assistants. The expansion has been particularly noteworthy in the United Kingdom, where they constitute nearly 40 percent of the school workforce (Department for Children, Schools and Families, 2009).

In England and Wales TAs have a direct instructional role and spend more time interacting with pupils than assisting teachers with administrative and clerical tasks (Department for Children, Schools and Families, 2009). The expectation of government is that they should have a direct impact on pupil attainment. The results of a national evaluation of the impact of aides on student achievement raise serious doubts about the effectiveness of this expenditure (Blatchford, Bassett, Brown, Martin, Russell, & Webster, 2010). Students with more TA support made either no more or significantly less academic progress than similar students with less of such support. These findings held true across English, math, and science and across four elementary and five high school grade levels. The results were not explained by students' background, prior achievement, or special needs status. Although there is no comparable U.S. study, the research that is available raises similar questions about the academic impact of aides in regular classrooms (Gerber, Finn, Achilles, & Boyd-Zaharias, 2001).

This research provides another significant challenge to widely accepted assumptions about the types of resources that will benefit student learning. More adults in classrooms may support the classroom teacher in managing a more diverse range of student needs, but such support does not translate into benefits for students unless the support persons have high-level pedagogical skills. Although the TA role in England and Wales did involve individual assistance with academic work, the results of this study show that the assistance was not sufficient to make a difference to student progress. Indeed, in most cases it retarded that progress by segregating the supported students within the classroom from the regular curriculum and the instructional guidance and expertise of the classroom teacher. The interaction between aides and their students was largely focused on completing tasks rather than on understanding the concepts and learning the skills that the tasks were intended to promote. The combination of the inadequate pedagogical training of the aides plus the shift in instructional responsibility from the classroom teacher to the aides probably account for the negative results. The aides became an alternative rather than an additional source of instructional guidance for students (Blatchford, Bassett, Brown, Martin, Russell, & Webster, 2010). For more information about this research visit www.schoolsupportstaff.net.

The strategic resourcing decision to be made by school leaders is whether teacher aides are an effective strategy for lifting student achievement, given the evidence that such investment will not pay off without substantial further investment in their pedagogical skills and knowledge. Under what conditions is this choice better than investing in the ability of classroom teachers to serve a more diverse range of students?

Strategic Decisions About Instructional Resources

Instructional resources include instructional programs, texts, documents describing curriculum progressions and standards, assessments, instructional software, templates, work sheets, and facilitators' manuals. Some resources are designed by teachers themselves, but many are designed by professional research and development organizations. The influence that school and district leaders exercise through their choice of instructional resources far outweighs the influence that they exercise through face-to-face interaction because their decisions about which resources to adopt shape the work of so many people. Organizational routines develop around the use of instructional resources, and over time these routines become part of the school culture. For example, the headings and categories on the parent report card determine what parents learn about their children's achievement; the classroom observation checklist shapes the practice of both the observed and the observer; and the protocols in the facilitators' handbook determine the focus and the structure of the professional learning activity.

Instructional resources, or *tools* as they are sometimes called, are concrete representations of ideas about how to achieve particular purposes (Spillane, 2006). Once we understand resources or tools as incorporating sets of ideas, we can ask questions about the quality of those ideas and about the quality of their concrete representation. This gives school leaders two broad criteria for evaluating the quality of their most important instructional resources:

- How valid are the ideas on which the resource or tool is based?
- How good is the design of the resource?

I call resources that satisfy both criteria *smart tools*—those that do not are *dumb tools* (Robinson & Timperley, 2007)!

The Validity of the Ideas

This first criterion evaluates the validity of the ideas on which the tool is based. It is useful to think of these ideas as a theory of action about how the purpose of the tool is achieved. A text that claims to teach mathematical reasoning is based on assumptions about how students learn to reason mathematically and about how teachers foster such learning by engaging students with a sequence of concepts and activities. Once the theory in the text is made explicit, its validity can be evaluated. Does the theory in the tool fit with our best evidence about how children develop conceptual understanding and learn to problem solve? Does it fit with teachers' experience about the types of activities that foster problem solving and reasoning? Does the balance in the text between computational fluency and problem solving seem appropriate to the development of mathematical reasoning?

A more direct way of evaluating validity of a tool is by seeking evidence about the consequences of its use. A reliable evidence base is rapidly developing about the effect of various types of instructional resources on student progress and achievement. One excellent source of such information is the *Best Evidence Encyclopedia* (www.bestevidence.org/) produced under the leadership of Bob Slavin at Johns Hopkins University in the United States and York University in England. The *Best Evidence Encyclopedia* provides reports comparing the effects of four different types of instructional resources on the math and reading achievement of elementary, middle, and high school students (Slavin, Cheung, Groff, & Lake, 2008; Slavin, Lake, Chambers, Cheung, & Davis, 2009). The four broad categories of resources are texts and curricula, instructional technology, professional development interventions into instructional processes, and instructional technology combined with interventions into instructional processes.

The conclusions these authors draw about what works are remarkably similar for both math and reading and for elementary and high school students. In summary, investments in new curricula, texts, and instructional technology are highly unlikely, on their own, to make a worthwhile difference to student achievement in either of these subjects. This generalization holds up across different types of text and across many different types of instructional technology. Simply introducing a new text or new instructional software is unlikely to lift achievement unless accompanied by professional development that changes teachers' daily instruction. Despite the massive investment by education systems in new software and hardware, there is now ample evidence that, unless it is embedded in a sound classroom program, additional investments in instructional technology will not deliver better student achievement.

Far more effective are those professional development interventions that change teachers' daily instruction by providing them with proven strategies for teaching reading and math. The more effective programs typically integrate subject-specific strategies with aspects of cooperative learning and metacognitive skills. These latter strategies help teachers lift student engagement by developing better independent and peer-assisted study skills.

In addition to reporting on the relative effectiveness of broad categories of instructional resources, the *Best Evidence Encyclopedia* also reports the evidence, when available, on the effectiveness of ready-made instructional packages for teaching reading and math. It notes, however, that many widely used resources have been subject to little rigorous evaluation. There are, for example, over one hundred middle and high school reading programs used in the United States for which no rigorous studies of effectiveness are available (Slavin, Cheung, Groff, & Lake, 2008).

The Quality of the Design

The second criterion for a smart tool concerns its design. Even though a tool incorporates a valid theory, it might still be a dumb tool if it is poorly constructed and hard to use. One of the best ways to evaluate this criterion is to listen to the reaction of current or future users. I had little idea of the importance of tool design until a colleague used criteria from research on instructional design to evaluate an earlier version of New Zealand's national curriculum in social studies (Aitken, 2005). In New Zealand, a curriculum is a broad set of guidelines, not a text, and teachers have to interpret the guidelines in order to develop their own lesson plans. One reason for the poor implementation of the social studies curriculum was the design of the guidelines themselves. For example, an analysis of the documents showed that in order to plan their lessons on national identity, teachers needed to consider three learning processes (including twelve component processes), two levels of achievement, six perspective statements, seven essential learning statements, four subject disciplines, eleven concepts, and three indicators of achievement! Fortunately, the complexity was somewhat reduced in the subsequent 2007 curriculum document (New Zealand Ministry of Education, 2007).

Table 4.1 describes and explains some design criteria that can be applied to the evaluation of many different types of instructional tools, particularly those that are intended to support changed teaching practice (Mayer & Moreno, 2003; Paas, Renkl, & Sweller, 2003).

Table 4.1   Some Criteria for the Design of Smart Tools

Criterion	Description of Criterion	Rationale for Criterion
Clear purpose	The tool is logically structured around a clear and unambiguous purpose.	Settling on a clear purpose makes the tool development process more difficult if the purpose is contested, but it is essential for the coherence of the document and for reducing the cognitive load on users.
Justifies need for change	The need for change and the principles underpinning it are clearly explained.	Comparing the old and the new practices deepens understanding of purpose and prevents the perception that there is nothing new.

Principles linked to examples	Abstract principles are clearly connected to spatially contiguous detail and examples.	Principles gain meaning from detailed examples, and spatial contiguity reduces cognitive load.
Misconception alerts	Possible misunderstandings are directly addressed.	Providing both positive and negative examples of the intended practices deepens understanding and reinforces required changes.
Cognitive load	The tool has high coherence and low complexity.	Working memory poses severe limits on users' abilities to understand and remember multiple interacting elements of a document. Complexity is reduced by including fewer elements and giving practical examples of how they can be integrated.
Alignment of text and visuals	Language and meaning of text are reinforced by tightly aligned visuals.	Ideas are clarified by alternative visual representations that are spatially contiguous to the relevant text and incorporate the same language, sequence, and relationships as the text.

It is interesting to note the similarity between some of the principles in this table and those that are discussed in the section on leading teacher change in Chapter Six. Whether leading change through the introduction of a new written resource or through face-to-face communication, it is important to be open about the reason for change. Equally important is an explicit comparison between current and future practices because teachers often believe they are already doing what the change requires.

Strategic Decisions About Instructional Time

Establishing a school culture in which instructional time is treated as a strategic resource is an important responsibility of school leadership because achievement is a function of both the *amount* and the *quality* of instruction. Without quality, longer school days, summer schools, and increased time spent on a particular subject waste student and teacher time (Cuban, 2008). Given adequate quality, however, increased time spent on a subject will raise achievement (Scheerens & Bosker, 1997).

There is wide variation in the amount of time students spend in school. A comparison across the ten largest U.S. school districts shows that students in Houston and Philadelphia spend 30 percent more time in school than students in the Chicago public schools (Miles & Frank, 2008). Some commentators believe that U.S. students fall behind in international achievement studies because they spend considerably less time than students in comparable higher-performing countries in academically rigorous subjects. Although there is still controversy about the effectiveness of the Blair government's literacy strategy in England (Tymms, 2004), one reason why it did lift achievement, at least initially, was that the highly structured literacy hour ensured that every English primary school child got at least one hour of literacy instruction a day.

Gaining an accurate understanding of how instructional time is currently used is an important initial step in becoming more strategic about the use of this resource. Miles and Frank (2008) provide a step-by-step guide to this analysis, which begins with determining the proportion of school time students spend in several different types of instruction. The main categories they use are

1. Instructional time—the total number of hours of instruction
   a. Instructional time in core academics—hours spent in English, math, social studies, and foreign languages
   b. Instructional time in noncore academic subjects—time in all other courses

2. Support and enrichment—other supervised study time, such as tutorials, enrichment, advisory periods

3. Maintenance and unassigned time—lunch breaks, unsupervised study time

4. Release time—time when students are excused from school, for example, for work

Leaders often find the results eye-opening because they now realize the big picture implications of their prior decisions. The results show that students at all levels "typically spend less than 75 percent of their time at school on instruction and secondary schools spend less than 50 percent of time on core academics. . . . Organizing time in this way is a choice, not an imperative" (Miles & Frank, 2008, p. 77).

Once the distribution of instructional time is made visible, leaders can evaluate its consequences for the achievement of learning goals. Although more refined analyses are needed than can be discussed here, the key questions are whether instructional time should be reorganized to provide more high-quality instruction to students who need it and larger blocks of time to their teachers so they can develop strategies for accelerating the learning of their students. Miles and Frank's (2008) book includes numerous case studies of schools that have achieved both these changes by reorganizing the schedule and introducing more flexible forms of student grouping.

If schoolwide data show numerous students failing to reach proficiency targets, then an extension of instructional time in core subjects along with attention to instructional quality may be required. There is little point in extending instructional time, however, if the existing time is not carefully protected. Protecting instructional time means minimizing disruption to scheduled classes through pull-out programs, special events, test preparation, and general end-of-year or end-of-semester slowdowns. It also means reducing interruptions to classes through announcements and other administrative intrusions. Instructional time in core subjects can also be eroded, particularly in the elementary grades, by teachers' choices about what to teach.

High-quality instructional time is a precious resource for students who have little out-of-school access to the school curriculum. Although middle class parents can provide access to this curriculum at home, children from working class, minority, and new immigrant communities are much less likely to have such access. Although all students' achievement tends to drop during the summer break, that of students from high-poverty backgrounds drops considerably more (Cooper, Nye, Charlton, Lindsay, & Greathouse, 1996). One possible cause is the lower engagement of working class students in literacy activities during the three-month vacation. Another possibility is that a weak academic focus at the beginning of the new school year particularly disadvantages working class students. The former could be addressed by engaging parents and students in summer school reading preparation and activities. The latter could be addressed by ensuring that teachers have the capacity to assess students and help them recover any lost ground in the first month of the new school year (Hattie, 2009).

The expansion of school time through summer school and after-school programs is a strategy that has been adopted by many systems to increase the amount of instruction. Evaluations of summer school and after-school programs deliver consistent messages about what makes them more effective: tight alignment with the classroom curriculum; an academic focus; high-quality teaching by trained personnel, whether or not they are certified teachers; monitoring of attendance; and strong links with families and community (Odden, 2009). In short, without quality instruction, extensions to the school day or school year will not benefit students.

Instructional Time and Pull-Out Programs

Even with attention to instructional quality and extended instructional time in core subjects, there will be students who struggle to reach proficiency levels. Perhaps the most common way of providing extra services to these students is through pull-out programs, many of which are funded through additional state and federal funding. The expansion of such services in the United States has radically altered the balance between resourcing of regular and special educational programs. For example, in 1967 80 percent of school spending supported regular programs, and by 1996 this figure had dropped to just over 50 percent (Miles & Frank, 2008).

The problem, according to Miles and Frank (2008), is that "providing isolated specialized services drains dollars from other students and teachers and creates incentives to categorize or over-diagnose students as having special needs" (p. 8). Frequent referral of students reduces the responsibility of classroom teachers to teach *all* their students and the responsibility of their leaders to help them to do so. As pull-out services grow, expectations change about the range of diversity that will be catered to in the regular classroom and the skill sets of teachers progressively narrow. An administrative machinery for referrals and monitoring develops, which further drains resources from the regular classroom. In a bid to win and retain resources, schools can accumulate a plethora of additional programs that fragment the curriculum and drain both teacher and student time. As one set of funds dries up, leaders feel duty bound to seek new funds in order to retain existing programs and the staff that deliver them.

The barriers to changing these patterns are formidable because many of the students who receive pull-out programs do so in accordance with individual education plans (IEPs) that are nego-tiated under federal special education law. Changing such plans requires parents to agree to a new assessment of the student and to any revised plan. Thus, changed provision for students with special learning needs requires not only challenging school norms about how such services are provided but also educating parents about why alternatives to pull-out programs are worth considering.

One can readily understand, therefore, why school leaders might conclude that the combination of federal law, parental lobbying for separate provision, teachers' capacity to cater to increased diversity, and the administrative complexity of a change would make it futile to even attempt such a change.

Nevertheless, not all students in pull-out programs are subject to IEP contracts, and Miles and Frank's cases show that change is possible. The point is not to pit "in-class" against "out-of-class" provision but rather to reallocate resources to provide a hierarchy of services for struggling students that begins with in-class support for their teachers and becomes progressively more intensive and specialized when prior levels of support prove insufficient.

Many school districts that have dramatically improved student achievement have included such a staged approach within their reform strategies (Odden, 2009). The first stage involves supporting classroom teachers to quickly identify and provide extra help to struggling students. If this is not sufficiently effective, the next stage is for a tutor to provide extra help, either by working alongside the classroom teacher or in a pull-out setting. The research on tutoring suggests it should focus on the specific concepts and skills that are difficult for the student and that the tutor should be specifically trained in teaching that material (Gordon, 2009). The size of the tutorial group should be responsive to the level of student difficulty, with only the highest-need students receiving an individual approach. The aim is to help students early with their specific learning difficulties rather than to provide more general ongoing support. In these successful districts the time for tutoring was typically taken from electives—the rationale for this difficult choice was the school and district priorities for higher performance in core academic subjects. The next level of support comprised a range of different extended day and summer school activities. The final stage of support was "to provide even more additional service under the federal and state programs geared to students with identified disabilities, but all the previous services are options to be provided before a student is put into a program specifically geared to a disability" (Odden, 2009, p. 87).

In summary, there are a number of principles underpinning the provision of extra instructional services: resource these services in ways that strengthen rather than undermine the capacity of classroom teachers to be successful with diverse students; tailor the services flexibly according to the specific needs of the students; focus the content of the instruction on the particular concepts and skills that the student is having trouble with; and staff the extra provision with teachers, tutors, or aides who are trained to teach that particular content.

Reflective Questions About Dimension Two Leadership

- Do school leaders challenge the assumption that improved learning requires additional resources?

- How open are school leaders to rethinking traditional patterns of allocating time, staffing, and money?

- Is staff recruitment based on an analysis of the match between student needs and current staff capability?

- What emphasis is given by school and district leaders in the selection of instructional programs and resources to rigorous evaluations of their effectiveness?

- Have leaders responsible for creating a timetable analyzed the consequences of their decisions for the amount of instruction students receive in their areas of highest need?

- Does support for struggling students begin with expert help for their classroom teachers?

Summary

When clear goals are in place, leaders can be strategic about allocating and organizing money, time, and staffing in ways that increase the chance of success. An initial step in taking a more strategic approach to the organization of these resources is to analyze and evaluate existing patterns of resource allocation in terms of alignment to learning goals and research evidence about the relative effectiveness of different types of programs. Even though staffing is constrained by contractual obligations, high-quality, proactive, and school- and district-based recruitment, retention, and replacement policies can improve teacher quality. High-quality teachers need to work with high-quality instructional resources. An increasingly rich evidence base shows that investments in instructional resources that include structured professional learning components are more effective than investments in instructional technology or new curricula. It is improvement in the quality of daily classroom practice that has the most powerful impact on student progress. When additional instructional time is needed for students who are still struggling, it is most effective when it is tightly aligned to the classroom program, based on students' specific learning challenges, and delivered by trained personnel, whether or not they are certified teachers.

5

Dimension Three
Ensuring Quality Teaching

Everywhere he spoke, Sonny Donaldson, superintendent of Aldine school district in Texas, repeated the same message: "The main thing is to keep the main thing the main thing." The main thing was learning, and by that he meant the learning of all students and student groups at equally high levels (Skrla, Scheurich, & Johnson, 2000). The challenge for leaders was to focus on learning and to sustain that focus in the face of myriad distractions.

Donaldson's aphorism captures the current emphasis on instructional leadership *and* the difficulty of meeting it. Instructional leadership is directed at the improvement of teaching and learning through leaders' involvement in the coordination and evaluation of the instructional program (Alig-Mielcarek & Hoy, 2005; Hallinger, 2005).

When the concept of instructional leadership was first introduced in the early 1980s, the assumption was made that it was the responsibility of the principal. The exclusive focus on the principal reinforced a heroic view of the role that few were able to live up to. As Hallinger (2005) comments, "Instructional leaders led from a combination of expertise and charisma. These were hands-on principals, hip-deep in curriculum and instruction . . . and unafraid of working directly with teachers on the improvement of teaching and learning. Descriptions of these principals tended towards a heroic view of their capabilities that often spawned feelings ranging from inadequacy to guilt among the vast majority of principals who wondered why they had such difficulty fitting into this role expectation" (p. 224).

Instructional leadership is performed by all teachers who have some responsibility, beyond their own classrooms, for the quality of learning and teaching. Indeed, the concept of *shared* instructional leadership accurately conveys the reality of how this work is organized in schools (Marks & Printy, 2003). The principal is an instructional leader and a leader of instructional leaders.

The Effect of Ensuring Quality Teaching on Student Outcomes

Instructional leadership embraces aspects of all five dimensions described in Figure 1.1, but at its heart is the dimension that is the subject of this chapter—leadership through ensuring quality teaching. The meta-analysis described in Chapter One showed that, on average, this leadership dimension has a moderate (0.42) impact on student outcomes. The measures used in the nine studies that contributed to this dimension included four different ways in which leadership ensures the quality of teaching.

First, the leadership of high-performing schools is distinguished by its active oversight and coordination of the instructional program (Heck, Larsen, & Marcoulides, 1990). This includes coordinating the curriculum across year levels and working with staff to develop progressions of teaching objectives in particular subjects (Heck, Marcoulides, & Lang, 1991).

Second, in high-performing schools, teachers report that their leaders are actively involved in collegial discussions of instructional matters, including how instruction affects student achievement (Heck, Marcoulides, & Lang, 1991).

Third, the degree of leader involvement in classroom observation and subsequent feedback is also associated with higher-performing schools. Teachers in such schools report that their leaders set and adhere to clear performance standards for teaching (Andrews & Soder, 1987), make regular classroom observations, and provide feedback that helps them improve (Bamburg & Andrews, 1991; Heck, 1992).

Fourth, there was greater emphasis in high-performing schools on ensuring that staff systematically monitored student progress (Heck, 1992) and that test results were used for the purpose of program improvement (Heck, Marcoulides, & Lang, 1991).

This evidence points to the importance of coordinating the instructional program, providing useful feedback to teachers, and using data on student progress to improve the instructional program. In the rest of this chapter I discuss three big ideas to support leaders in the exercise of these responsibilities. The coordination of the instructional program requires an understanding of instructional program coherence. Useful feedback to teachers requires a defensible concept of effective teaching, and data-driven instructional improvement requires a culture of evidence-based inquiry.

Leadership That Develops a Coherent Instructional Program

The coherence of an instructional program matters for students and teachers. Students achieve more in schools with more coherent instructional programs (Newmann, Smith, Allensworth, & Bryk, 2001). Teachers develop stronger professional communities when they have a common approach to teaching and learning (Bryk, Sebring, Allensworth, Luppescu, & Easton, 2010). I develop these ideas by first explaining the concept of instructional program coherence and how it promotes student and teacher learning. I then outline some leadership strategies for developing coherence and caution against pursuing coherence in ways that curb inquiry into its effectiveness.

A Coherent Instructional Program

A coherent instructional program has three components (Newmann, Smith, Allensworth, & Bryk, 2001):

- An instructional framework, comprising curriculum, instructional strategies, and assessments, that is co-ordinated within and between grade levels. Within grades, coherence ensures students at the same grade level get equivalent access to subject content, regardless of teacher assignment. Between grades, coordination ensures a progression of increasingly difficult subject matter. Instructional support in the form of extra tutoring, remedial programs, and parent involvement uses the common instructional framework. Instructional frameworks can be developed by external providers or developed within a school as a result of collaborative inquiry into the effects of different teaching approaches.

- The school's culture and organization supports and requires the use of the framework. Administrators use commitment to and competence in the use of the framework as criteria for the recruitment and evaluation of teachers. Professional development opportunities are designed to give teachers sustained opportunities to critically examine, implement, and refine their use of the framework.

- The school allocates resources to support the sustained use of the instructional framework and to avoid conflicting initiatives.

In essence, instructional program coherence refers to a common instructional framework for the pursuit of one or more core academic goals and the organizational and resourcing procedures that support its sustained use. It is worth noting at this point that a coherent instructional program does not imply a tightly scripted, "teacher-proof" curriculum. Considerable skill is needed on the part of teachers to diagnose student needs against grade-level expectations and apply appropriately differentiated instructional strategies. That is why collaborative professional learning is an important component of the development and implementation of a coherent instructional framework.

How Instructional Coherence Promotes Achievement

Instructional coherence works because it supports how students learn. We know that students learn and remember more when key ideas are presented in ways that connect with their prior knowledge and experience (Bransford, Brown, & Cocking, 2000). We also know that exposure to multiple representations of the same idea over a relatively short period of time—say a unit of work spanning ten days—promotes their learning (Nuthall & Alton-Lee, 1993). Learning opportunities that meet these conditions are more likely to be found in instructional programs that are planned around a progression of learning objectives that are mapped onto an instructional calendar. A common instructional framework means that teachers reinforce the same ideas, use similar vocabulary for communicating those ideas, know how to make links with what has gone before, and are guided in their efforts by common assessments. If students' learning opportunities are integrated and cumulative, rather than fragmented and rushed, students are more likely to be engaged and successful.

The same logic applies to teacher learning. Teachers are more likely to improve their practice with professional learning opportunities that are integrated and cumulative, and that convey consistent messages about how to teach. With increased coherence, the learning agenda for staff changes from one that is a mile wide and an inch deep to one that is focused, sustained, and shared. In addition, their learning is supported by their colleagues who share a commitment to the instructional framework and by administrative procedures and resource allocations that are aligned to the framework. Teachers' motivation is greater when they are confident that the focus of their professional learning will not change with the next change of administrator or funding opportunity. In short, the second reason why students learn more in coherent programs is that their teachers are learning together about how to teach the things they are supposed to be learning.

How Leaders Increase Instructional Coherence

Developing an instructional framework that includes the three components is a lengthy and complex business. It might be helpful, therefore, to establish priorities about which subjects require greater coherence. An obvious rationale is to give priority to those subjects in which schoolwide assessments show below-expected achievement levels. The source of increased coherence may be a well-proven program such as those discussed in Chapter Three or a program that has been developed by teachers themselves through their collaborative and evidence-informed study of the impact of their own practice. More is said about how to develop the strong professional communities needed to do this work in Chapter Six.

Many aspects of school organization are not conducive to increasing the coherence of instruction. Under what is often referred to as the "egg crate" system of school organization, teaching becomes a private practice with each teacher making his or her own decisions about how to interpret and teach the curriculum (Darling-Hammond, 2006). Increased autonomy means less sharing because wide variation in teaching practice makes it difficult to identify which teachers need help and which teachers have relevant expertise.

Shifting from a private to a more public teacher culture requires different strategies depending on the strength of the egg-crate culture in a particular school. If this culture is strong, a good starting point may be the "constructive problem talk" I introduced in the discussion of goal setting (Chapter Three). You could lead a discussion about why you believe the current level of autonomy has become counterproductive for achieving the goals and values that teachers already espouse. For example, you could explain how the price of autonomy is less teamwork and less support in solving difficult teaching problems. You could also explain the research on program coherence and why you think it is applicable to your school.

In seeking staff reaction to your views, you are likely to encounter arguments about the loss of autonomy that comes with more systematic shared practice. It is often assumed that any such loss of autonomy is undesirable because it somehow reduces the professionalism of teachers. Although there is no question that increased coherence means reduced autonomy, it does not necessarily imply decreased professionalism. Doctors are seen as professionals because they have mastered complex sets of shared diagnostic and treatment practices. They exercise their judgment about how those procedures are to be applied in any individual case and are held accountable for those judgments. They need sufficient autonomy to exercise those judgments, but by virtue of being professional their autonomy to diagnose and treat as they please is massively constrained.

When dealing with objections to loss of teacher autonomy it is worth remembering one of the lessons from my earlier discussion of problem solving (Chapter Two). Teacher autonomy is only *one* of several conditions that need to be satisfied in determining the desirable level of instructional coherence. Teachers need sufficient autonomy to exercise their professional judgment about how to use the framework and to contribute to evaluative discussions about its adequacy. But that autonomy should also be constrained by the need to ensure effective teaching practice—that is, practice under which *all* students achieve to a high level. Another important requirement might be to reduce teacher stress and sense of isolation. *Effective problem solving involves finding a solution that sufficiently satisfies all these solution requirements.*

The Need for a Theory of Quality Teaching

Every time leaders observe classrooms, give feedback to teachers, oversee planning, or make recommendations for improvement, they operate from an implicit or explicit theory of quality teaching. In some cases, what counts as quality teaching is specified by a standardized program that the school has adopted. However, because standardized programs typically account for only a small proportion of total teaching time, it is leaders' own beliefs about what counts as quality teaching that inform many of their instructional leadership practices. The validity of these beliefs is central to the effectiveness of their leadership of the improvement of teaching and learning. In the following, I briefly outline two views of quality teaching that I believe to be inadequate and then offer a third view that I believe to be more defensible. I show how each of these views could affect the evaluative judgments leaders make about the quality of teaching.

Two Inadequate Views of Quality Teaching

Most judgments about the quality of teaching are based on a preferred teaching style. Style can refer to a teaching approach (for example, the use of a particular pedagogy such as direct instruction); to personal attributes (for example, the use of humor, displaying warmth, or adopting a businesslike manner); or to particular instructional skills (for example, providing an overview, using visuals, or explaining clearly).

Teachers and leaders typically have strong views about which style they prefer. In New Zealand and Australia, at least, a highly participative style focused on independent student inquiry and creative activity is much more likely to be preferred than a more formal didactic style, especially if that style is closely aligned to standardized assessments. The formal style is usually criticized because of

- The narrowness of the learning outcomes being taught and assessed

- The students' lack of enjoyment of the lessons
- Students' choosing not to continue in the subject

Notice that each of these criticisms is testable by inquiring into the assumed consequences of the style. Leaders who fear that such a formal style may stifle student creativity and interest in the subject should inquire into that possibility rather than assume its truth in any particular instance. If leaders omit the inquiry and assume the validity of their style-based evaluation, they are guilty of discriminating against their more formal teachers (Scriven, 1990).

Those who make such criticisms might argue that their evaluations are justified by the ample research evidence that shows that a formal style does have the consequences they claim. The problem with this argument is that, even if this research generalization were true, it expresses a probability rather than a certainty that formal teaching will lead to these negative consequences. The generalization is useful because it alerts us to possible negative consequences, but the reality of those consequences eventuating in any particular teaching context must be tested rather than assumed. That is why evaluations based on teaching style are flawed.

Results-based evaluation is a second unsatisfactory approach to the evaluation of teaching quality. Although, as I shall argue in the next section, student results provide one crucial source of information about the quality of teaching, they do not, *in themselves*, constitute an adequate basis for making judgments of quality. Because the most powerful predictor of a child's current achievement is his or her prior achievement, "value added" rather than absolute measures of achievement are required to make judgments about a teacher's contribution to student learning. As I indicated in Chapter One when discussing leadership effectiveness, the bottom line for leaders and teachers is the *difference* they make to student learning, not the students' absolute level of achievement. But even when teachers (or leaders) appear to have made little difference, the data do not speak for themselves. Questions must always be asked about the causes of the students' progress or lack of it and the skill and effort being put into creating the conditions that are needed for improvement. If those efforts are of high quality, then over time the outcomes will improve.

Results-based evaluation of teaching is particularly problematic if the evaluation is used for formal accountability purposes. Holding teachers accountable for results, especially if associated with sanctions and incentives, can destroy trust, teamwork, and the development of collective responsibility for student achievement. As I discussed in Chapter Two, conversations with teachers about teaching quality are a critical leadership responsibility, and students' work and results should be part of the discussion. In these conversations, the student data are used to inquire into students' learning needs and how well a teacher is meeting them rather than to make summative judgments about teaching quality. In the next section, I propose a more defensible theory of quality teaching that evaluates teaching on the basis of how teachers provide opportunities to learn rather than how they conform to a given style or how their students achieve.

Quality Teaching as Providing Opportunities to Learn

Both the quantity and quality of teaching are critical determinants of what students learn in classrooms. These two aspects of teaching effectiveness are captured in the idea of "opportunities to learn"—a concept developed by the educational psychologist David Berliner (1987, 1990). In essence, *high-quality teaching maximizes the time that learners are engaged with and successful in the learning of important outcomes.* This concept provides a set of principles about teaching quality that have considerable practical relevance and do not prejudge the effectiveness of particular teaching styles or make simplistic use of student assessment data.

The central idea is how teachers use time allocated for particular subjects. In a forty-week school year about 160 hours are allocated for the teaching of a particular subject. There are numerous ways in which this allocated time can be eroded in terms of the quantity and quality of the learning opportunity. First, time can be lost through waiting for the learning activity to start because students or the teacher are late, because the resources are not yet available, or because the transition between activities is badly managed. One indicator of quality teaching is that routines are in place to minimize such wait time.

Second, time can be lost through misalignment between important intended learning outcomes and the lesson activities. In a unit of work on insects, for example, a teacher provides multiple opportunities to learn the characteristics of insects, including an art lesson in which students are asked to "be creative" and "use their imagination" in painting their insects. The teacher provides positive feedback on this basis and makes no comments about paintings that depict creatures that are not insects. At a more mundane level, lesson activities can be misaligned because learners spend their time drawing headings, coloring diagrams, and guessing the correct answer on work sheets rather than developing the intended conceptual understandings.

Third, even though wait time is minimized and lesson activities and teacher feedback are carefully aligned to the intended outcomes, students may not engage with the activities. Students are cognitively engaged when they are actively thinking about the material. It is important that being behaviorally engaged or "on-task" is not taken by teachers or their evaluators as equivalent to being cognitively engaged. The latter is best assessed by asking students what they are trying to learn and how they will know when they have been successful.

Cognitive engagement may be low because the material may assume prior knowledge that the students do not have, or conversely, may present ideas that students already know. Learners may be disengaged because they do not feel emotionally connected with the material, with the teacher, or both.

The fourth way in which time is lost is through persistent lack of success. Quality teaching provides learning opportunities that are not only aligned to important learning outcomes and well matched to students' prior knowledge and interests, but also designed to promote success. This does not mean that all failure is to be avoided, because mastering important learning outcomes often requires considerable intellectual effort and persistence, and these are qualities that teachers should nurture. A key to promoting success is early detection of students' misunderstandings because such misunderstandings subvert the learning the teacher intends the students to gain from the lesson activities (Nuthall & Alton-Lee, 1993). Teachers' feedback to students should attend to the content of their understanding in addition to the correctness of their answers.

In summary, quality teaching involves maximizing the time that students spend engaged with and being successful in the learning of important outcomes. This means that leaders' judgments about the quality of teaching are based on the four aspects listed in the left-hand side of Table 5.1. The questions in the right-hand column suggest the type of inquiry that leaders can make in conversations with teachers about each aspect of providing opportunities to learn.

Table 5.1   Questions for Inquiry into the Quality of Teaching

Four Aspects of Opportunity to Learn	Questions for Inquiry into Each Aspect
1. The importance of the outcomes being pursued	*What are the intended learning outcomes for this lesson or unit of work? Why are they important for these students at this time?*
2. Alignment of the activities and resources with the outcomes	*How are these resources or activities intended to help the students achieve the anticipated outcomes?*

3. The behavioral and cognitive engagement of students	*How did these materials and activities build on the relevant prior knowledge, interests, and experience of these groups or individual students?* *How well were the students focused on the big ideas in the lesson?*
4. The students' success on the outcomes	*What do you know about how the students understood the big ideas?* *What information do you have about how they achieved the intended learning outcomes?* *What are their remaining misunderstandings?*

The opportunity-to-learn approach to quality teaching provides a set of broad principles rather than a behavioral checklist and thus allows many different styles and pedagogical strategies. It also promotes inquiry into the impact of preferred styles and strategies on the engagement and success of students.

Building a Culture of Evidence-Based Inquiry and Improvement

Quality teaching is developed through cycles of inquiry and action designed to increase the impact of teaching on the engagement and success of students. Although evidence about student achievement is an essential resource for such inquiry, the challenge for most school leaders is not the availability of such evidence but creating a culture in which it is used for the purpose of improvement.

Sometimes teachers are skeptical about whether the assessment data they are working with really capture what they believe to be educationally important. At other times, they doubt the reliability and rigor of the evidence they are working with or, alternatively, they see its technical sophistication as a barrier to their understanding. In low-trust environments, in which teachers fear that data could be used against them, public discussion of assessment data may be seen as threatening and risky, triggering defensiveness rather than learning. Experienced teachers may question whether engaging with data can add anything to what they already know about their students.

Building a culture of evidence-based inquiry requires a balance between advocating its use and genuine responsiveness to such concerns. The three capabilities described in Chapter Two are important for finding this balance, so examples of their use in building a culture of evidence-based inquiry are provided throughout this section.

The importance of using data is repeated so often that it is assumed that everyone knows why it is important. A common understanding of purpose should not be assumed, however, because there are many possible uses for data and some of them have little to do with increasing the impact of teaching on the engagement and success of students. The purpose of data use, as I discuss it in this section, is to assist individual and collaborative reflection on the quality of decisions about how and what to teach and the quality of decisions about the administrative and organizational supports for such teaching.

Linking Data to Decision Making

Data are more likely to be valued and used when teachers understand how they can inform particular decision-making and problem-solving processes. When data are treated as a resource for decision making, the focus remains on the quality of the professional judgment of staff. Data calibrate but do not replace professional judgment. They need to be interpreted in terms of the context in which they were collected, including the opportunity the students had to learn the material, and with reference to relevant benchmarks and standards.

Leaders and teachers report that issues of relevance, accessibility, time, and capability present barriers to their use of student assessment data (Earl & Fullan, 2003; Park & Datnow, 2009). The following strategies address these barriers by strengthening the links between data and decision making.

Relevance

Leaders can mitigate the relevance issue by determining the type of data that could or should inform particular decisions. If the decision is about progress toward the school's strategic goals, then are data available that can inform judgments about that progress? If decisions are needed about the retention of particular programs, are data available about the learning of students in the program and, if possible, of a comparable group of students who experienced a different one? Are the data about teachers' own students helpful for making instructional decisions? Relevant data are frequently collected but not collated or analyzed in ways that make them available to decision makers (Robinson, Phillips, & Timperley, 2002). The reasons are multiple: school routines ensure that assessment data are collected and reported, but there are no equivalent routines for collaborative discussion of the data, or teachers may be insufficiently trained in their interpretation or lack the time to study them. Data overload can be reduced by being ruthless about not collecting data that are not used—or if their collection is required, trying to find a use beyond that of compliance with external reporting requirements. The goal is to ensure that data that are collected are used and that data that are not used are not collected.

Accessibility

When data are tightly coupled to decision opportunities, their format and timing are responsive to the requirements of the relevant decision makers. Strong feedback loops are required between those responsible for generating the data and the users so that solutions to problems of format, timeliness, accessibility, privacy, and other technical constraints can be found while still meeting the requirements of users. Teachers complain about the technical limitations of the systems they use, the time involved in data entry, and a lack of alignment between different data recording systems (Park & Datnow, 2009). Overcoming these technical challenges requires coordinated and sustained work by state, district, and school leaders and technical specialists (Wayman & Stringfield, 2006). School leaders need a strong voice in explaining what they need and why so that a partnership approach is taken to building a data infrastructure that serves the needs of leaders and teachers as well as district officials.

Time to Use the Data

Leaders are often urged to reorganize timetables to create time for teachers to collaborate on data use. Although this may be desirable, a decision-linked approach suggests a different framing of this concern. A prior step is to identify the decisions that the data would inform and then ask how those decisions are currently being made. If the relevant decision is made in an existing meeting, then time has already been allocated. The problem is not time but learning how to insert data into the current decision-making process. This takes us to the next barrier—learning how to interpret data.

Capacity to Use Data

A major barrier to the use of data is capacity to interpret them. Although there may be a case for courses in data literacy (Earl & Katz, 2002), a decision-linked approach suggests that such capacity building should be contextualized in particular decision arenas. Whether or not teachers have the capacity to make good instructional decisions on the basis of assessments of their students' reading will depend not only on their ability to interpret the data but also on the extent to which the assessments are linked to a teaching progression. When assessment tools lack such links, then a far greater capacity is needed to use the information to inform teaching decisions because it requires deep knowledge of the subject and its pedagogy as well as knowledge of the assessment itself.

Using Evidence to Foster Inquiry Habits of Mind

Learning from evidence requires a deeply personal appreciation of how it is essential to one's professional learning and growth. Without such appreciation and the associated skills, data use becomes an exercise in evaluating other people rather than in collective learning and improvement. Leaders who espouse the values of an open-to-learning conversation (Chapter Two) will recognize data as a resource for increasing the validity of their own and others' assumptions about their students, how to teach them, and the effectiveness of current practice.

The following extract from an account of district-driven reform in a U.S. urban high school provides a powerful lesson in how leaders can use constructive problem talk (Chapter Three) to confront norms and assumptions that are counterproductive to inquiry about how to increase the impact of teaching on student engagement and success.

In 2003, faculty members at Lincoln Public School, located in the heart of a large urban city, confronted some difficult news: the state identified the school as needing program improvement. With a student population that was over 95 percent children of immigrant backgrounds who also qualified for the Free and Reduced Lunch Program, teachers and administrators put forth their best effort to help students learn. At the same time, the overwhelming refrain heard from staff members when pushed to incorporate higher standards or produce improvements in student performance was, "Look at our kids and where they come from. We can't change who they are" or, "We're doing the best we can. It's not us . . . it's the _____ (e.g., parents, students' behavior, lack of support from the administration, or lack of resources)." The truth was that the majority of teachers were fulfilling their professional responsibilities to their utmost ability. Some even went above and beyond. . . .

To get past the "we can't" attitude, the administrators shared student achievement data from a neighborhood school serving the same types of students. Despite having the same student population, the same number of students, and the same resource concerns, the comparison school was recognized as a high-performing school at the top of the state's rankings. At the faculty meeting where this [sic] data were shared, there was complete silence. For once, the tendency to blame kids or their families was challenged by the superior student performance of a similar school. For once, teachers were forced to consider that children and their families might not be the problem. For the first time, space was created for teachers and administrators to reflect on what made the difference. At that moment, there were infinite possibilities for change and growth. [Park, 2008, pp. 1–2]

Prior to this meeting, Lincoln teachers had interpreted the data about the low performance of their students through their taken-for-granted assumptions about its causes and their own capacity to make a bigger difference. The data provided by the district administrators promoted inquiry because they directly challenged those beliefs. If another similar school, experiencing the same barriers to success as they were, had achieved dramatically different results, then their explanations were at best incomplete.

Studying data does not prompt learning unless you have the desire and the skills to use the data to test the validity of your thinking about what it means. Social psychologists have established that given a choice, people are more likely to ignore than engage with information that is not supportive of their existing beliefs (Hart, Albarracin, Eagly, Brechan, Lindberg, & Merrill, 2009).

This is more a function of our limited information-processing capacities than of our character but, nevertheless, it presents a considerable obstacle for the development of an inquiry culture. The example of Lincoln High School shows that if data are going to interrupt our bias toward confirming rather than testing our views, then discussions of data need to be treated as opportunities for offering *and testing* hypotheses about what the data might mean.

One tool that leaders I have worked with have found useful for interrupting taken-for-granted assumptions about teaching and learning is the ladder of inference. Originally developed by Argyris and Schön (1974), it depicts how our prior experience and belief systems shape what we notice, how we interpret what we have noticed, and how those interpretations then determine how we act. Figure 5.1 illustrates this automatic reasoning process in the context of the evaluation of a teacher's lesson. Years of experience in classrooms produce assumptions about what good

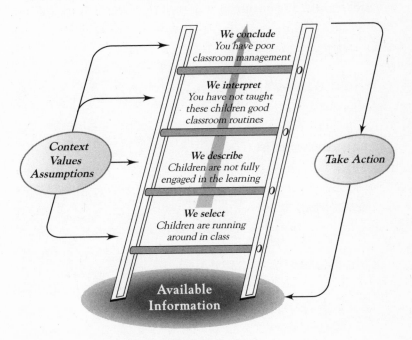

Figure 5.1   The Ladder of Inference

teaching looks like, and these shape what is noticed, how it is described, and the conclusions that are drawn about the effectiveness of a lesson. In an inquiry culture, both evaluator and teacher recognize that such conclusions are fallible and that the quality of thinking is improved by deliberate attempts to interrupt these otherwise automatic reasoning processes.

Creating an inquiry-based culture requires people to understand and accept the fallibility of their claims and to be skillful in checking the information and reasoning on which they are based. Learning how to observe and report what happens at the bottom of the ladder rather than immediately leaping to judgmental conclusions at the top of the ladder is a strong focus of the professional development process known as *instructional rounds* (City, Elmore, Fiarman, & Teitel, 2009). The purpose of this approach is to integrate a social practice of continuous improvement into the daily work of school leaders. Figure 5.2 presents some questions you can use to check the quality of your own thinking as you move up

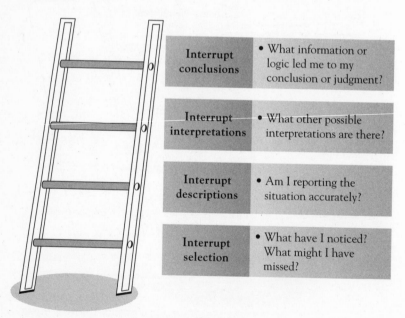

Interrupt conclusions	• What information or logic led me to my conclusion or judgment?
Interrupt interpretations	• What other possible interpretations are there?
Interrupt descriptions	• Am I reporting the situation accurately?
Interrupt selection	• What have I noticed? What might I have missed?

Figure 5.2   Questions for Checking the Validity of Inferences

the ladder of inference. They can also be used, with slight alteration, to help others to do the same.

An evidence-based culture of inquiry treats all knowledge claims as fallible and pays particular attention to the validity of those that inform decisions that have important consequences for children's and teachers' lives. Although high-quality, relevant, and accessible data provide an invaluable resource for decision making, the quality of those decisions is ensured not by the data but by the knowledge, inquiry values, and interpersonal respect that educators bring to data discussion and interpretation.

Reflective Questions About Dimension Three Leadership

- To what extent is the teaching of [specify subject] coordinated both within and across grade levels?

- To what extent is the teaching of [specify subject] informed by a common instructional framework?

- Do teachers and the leadership group have shared views about effective teaching and learning? What research or other evidence are those views based on?

- What proportion of our assessments are measuring things that teachers really value?

- How much data do we collect that are not used? Can we use such data in instructionally productive ways?

- What are the barriers our teachers experience to using assessment data for instructional purposes? What are leaders doing to reduce these barriers?

- How effective is our leadership team in using the ladder of inference to test and check our important assumptions?

Summary

The third dimension of student-centered leadership involves ensuring the quality of teaching through activities such as coordinating the instructional program, providing useful feedback to teachers, and using data on student progress to improve the instructional program. Such coordination requires an understanding of instructional program coherence and of how to achieve it in contexts in which teachers might expect to make more autonomous decisions about what and how to teach. Because many administrative routines are based on an implicit or explicit theory of effective teaching, it is important that leaders can articulate and reflect critically on what they mean by the concept. I argued that notions of effective teaching based on a preferred style or on student outcomes are both problematic. A third approach based on the quantity and quality of opportunities to learn was explained. Although leaders are urged to use student data for the purpose of improvement, the barriers to their use are often understated. Strategies were described about how to increase data use through stronger links between data and decisions and through inquiry into the validity of taken-for-granted assumptions.

6

Dimension Four
Leading Teacher Learning and Development

The public's expectations for higher standards, more equitable performance on those standards, and accountability for making progress toward them are likely to persist. They are part of the policy platforms of competing political parties and justified by an appeal to values that is hard to argue with. Although there will continue to be debate about what standards are appropriate and how to measure progress toward them, the drive for excellence and equity will endure.

It is increasingly clear that achieving these policy goals requires a great deal more than manipulation of accountability systems. Accountability, like goal setting, is a motivational mechanism that presumes the capacity to attain the relevant standard of performance. Increased accountability should be matched by increased commitment to build the capacity required to meet new performance expectations. I like the proposal of Richard Elmore (2004) to reframe top-down performance accountability as a reciprocal two-way process: "For every increment of performance I require of you, I have a responsibility to provide you with the additional capacity to produce that performance" (p. 89).

In this chapter, I discuss how leaders can build capacity in their schools by *integrating doing the work with learning how to improve the work*. Recent research evidence provides good guidance about the types of professional learning opportunities that change teacher practice in ways that improve the learning and achievement of the participating teachers. It also provides guidance about the qualities of school organization and teacher culture that support a shared and sustained focus on improvement. Because the three leadership capabilities described in Chapter Two are essential for effective leadership of teacher learning, this chapter provides extensive discussion and illustration of how they work in the context of leading teacher learning for the purpose of improvement.

The Effect of the Leadership of Teacher Learning on Student Outcomes

The most powerful way that school leaders can make a difference to the learning of their students is by promoting and participating in the professional learning and development of their teachers. The average impact (0.84) of these leadership practices on student outcomes was twice that of any other leadership dimension (Figure 1.1). I have described this dimension as promoting *and* participating in teacher learning because the leadership practices involved go well beyond organizing and resourcing the professional development program. Much of the evidence that contributed to this finding was about leaders themselves participating in the learning in the role of leader, learner, or both.

The contexts for their involvement were formal learning opportunities such as staff meetings or professional development activities and more informal opportunities such as hallway or office discussions about specific teaching problems. In both cases, in schools in which teachers reported more frequent or more effective leader involvement, students achieved more than in similar schools in which teachers reported less such involvement (Andrews & Soder, 1987; Bamburg & Andrews, 1991). In most but not all studies, the leader concerned was the principal.

Teachers in high-achieving schools were more likely to discuss teaching with their principals (Heck, Larsen, & Marcoulides, 1990; Heck, Marcoulides, & Lang, 1991) and see them as a source of instructional advice (Friedkin & Slater, 1994). This suggests that they were more accessible and more knowledgeable about instructional matters than their counterparts in otherwise similar lower-achieving schools. By contrast, the extent to which teachers identified principals as close personal friends or as participants in discussions did not distinguish the high- and low-performing schools.

I need to point out that the majority of this evidence came from studies of elementary schools. The notion of a high school principal being a source of instructional advice, at least in specialist subjects, is probably not realistic, but if one substitutes vice principal for instruction, curriculum chair, or head of subject department for principal, then the points are probably equally applicable to high school leadership.

Although these findings suggest the importance of this leadership dimension, they do not explain why it is associated with higher achievement or describe the knowledge and skills required to be an effective leader of professional learning. When I ask school leaders why they think these practices have such a large impact, they nearly always talk about their symbolic importance. They comment that the leader is modeling the importance of being a learner and that if a busy principal can give priority to the learning, then teachers may feel more inclined to do the same.

Although I agree with the symbolic importance of leader involvement, there are additional reasons for the impact of this leadership dimension. Leaders who participate with their staff are able to join in their professional discussions because they understand the concepts and the vocabulary associated with the new learning. Leaders' public endorsements of the importance of the learning or of the expertise of a facilitator are likely to be more credible because teachers know their leaders have firsthand experience of what they are endorsing (Matsumura, Sartoris, Bickel, & Garnier, 2009). But perhaps the most important reason for the effect is that direct involvement in professional learning enables leaders to learn in detail about the challenges the learning presents and the conditions teachers require to succeed. The leader can then take responsibility for ensuring these conditions are in place, whether they involve reorganization of a reading program, obtaining new resources, gaining agreement to classroom visits, or acceptance of regular feedback.

Teacher Learning as a Collective Endeavor

Effective professional development is a collective rather than individual endeavor because the work of teaching all students to succeed is a collective endeavor. This does not mean that any type of collective teacher learning is appropriate, because there are many ways in which it can be ineffective. Sometimes when teachers get together they reinforce counterproductive beliefs about what is wrong with students and spend little time examining their own practices (Lipman, 1997). At other times, teachers' divergent views about how to teach or their lack of skill in systematic exam-ination of problems of practice limit the learning they gain from their time together (Horn & Little, 2010). The fact that teachers in many schools do not work and learn as a team does not negate the importance of collective teacher learning. As I stated earlier, the most powerful predictor of a student's performance in a subject in any given year is what he or she learned in previous years. Because what any one teacher achieves, therefore, is critically dependent on the teaching quality of his or her colleagues, it makes sense that teachers take collective responsibility for their students, including helping each other learn how to reach shared goals.

The difficulty or reflection provides a second compelling reason to treat teacher learning as a collective endeavor. It is very hard to critique our own practice because we are likely to bring the reasoning that informs our practice to its evaluation. A well-functioning professional learning community will bring greater diversity of thinking to the analysis and resolution of particular teaching problems and thus help its members to break free of self-limiting assumptions and practices.

A third reason for treating teacher learning as a collective endeavor is that it builds the instructional program coherence I discussed in Chapter Five. If coherence is low, learning from and with others will be extremely difficult because teachers lack a shared language through which they can understand each other's practice. If everyone teaches differently and there are few standards for judging effectiveness, teachers cannot help one another, even if they wanted to, because they don't know enough about how their colleagues teach. When program coherence is higher, then teacher professional learning opportunities are likely to be more productive.

In effective professional learning communities (PLCs), members take collective responsibility for the learning of students. Newmann (1994) defines collective responsibility as "a sense of responsibility not only for one's own actions and students, but also for the actions of colleagues and other students in the school" (p. 2). In a well-functioning PLC, this means that teachers feel some obligation to help colleagues overcome their teaching problems and to share their own difficulties. Far from detracting from individual responsibility, collective and individual responsibilities are mutually supportive. If I know that I can get effective help from colleagues, then my confidence in my own teaching increases and I accept more responsibility for the learning and well-being of my students. Similarly, as my capacity and sense of responsibility increase, I take more responsibility for assisting my colleagues with their teaching problems.

As teachers work together, they develop shared understandings of the level of effort, commitment, and professionalism that they expect of each other. Such professional norms are a powerful form of professional accountability. In describing the qualities of effective professional communities, Kruse, Louis, and Bryk (1994) state that a strong collective focus on student learning is not enforced by rules but by mutually felt obligations to standards of instruction and learning. "Instead of obeying bureaucratic rules, faculty members act according to professional behavior and duty, which have been shown to be far stronger social control mechanisms" (p. 4).

School differences in the level of teachers' collective responsibility are predictive of student learning and achievement in elementary and high schools (Goddard, Hoy, & Hoy, 2000; Lee & Smith, 1996). In the high school study, students in higher-responsibility schools made larger gains over a two-year period in math, reading, science, and history than students in lower-responsibility schools that served similar communities (Lee & Smith, 1996). Just as significant was a second finding that those high schools with greater collective responsibility had a more even pattern of achievement across their students. The authors conclude that high-responsibility high schools are "not only more effective but more equalizing environments for students' learning where the learning of lower SES [socioeconomic status] students is similar to that of their higher-SES counterparts" (Lee & Smith, 1996, p. 129).

In summary, effective teacher learning is a collective endeavor that embraces every person who has responsibility for the instructional area under development. Well-functioning PLCs enhance the individual and collective responsibility that teachers accept for student learning. The most powerful way that leaders can promote collective responsibility is by providing professional learning opportunities that help teachers succeed with the students they find most difficult (Goddard, Hoy, & Hoy, 2000). In the next section I discuss what makes for a high-quality teacher-learning opportunity.

Knowledgeable Leadership of Teacher Learning

The appropriate ruler for assessing the effectiveness of professional learning and development is its impact on the learning of the students of the participating teachers. Although it is often important to know how satisfied teachers are with the learning opportunity or whether it has changed their teaching practice, neither of these indicators is a substitute for evaluating impact on students. Teachers may report high satisfaction with professional development that turns out to have little impact on their practice. Alternatively, they may faithfully implement new practices that do not have the intended effects on students (Timperley & Alton-Lee, 2008).

Effective leadership of teacher professional learning involves using evidence about student learning to inform decisions about what professional learning is needed, whether it is working, who it is working for, and when it should end. Effective planning of professional development involves, in addition, using the evidence about the types of professional learning that are most likely to change teaching practices in ways that benefit students (Elmore, 2004; Elmore & Burney, 1999; Timperley & Alton-Lee, 2008). This evidence suggests that effective professional development

- Serves identified student and teacher learning needs
- Focuses on the relationship between teaching and student learning
- Provides worthwhile content
- Integrates theory and practice
- Uses external expertise
- Provides multiple opportunities to learn

These six characteristics of effective professional development are briefly explained in the following.

Serves Identified Student and Teacher Learning Needs

Effective professional development is anchored in a deep understanding of the learning needs of students and an analysis of what teachers need to learn to meet those needs. "The core question in planning professional development is, 'What do we as teachers need to learn to promote the learning of our students?'"

(Timperley, 2008, p. 13). Because not every need can be met at once, leaders must decide which learning needs for which groups of students will drive the next professional development agenda. Once that purpose is clearly established, then it is possible to address related questions about who needs to be involved, how to evaluate the professional development, and how to embed it in the work of the relevant staff.

This student-driven approach is contrary to many current approaches to the setting of a professional development agenda. In some cases, the agenda is hijacked by district or school initiatives that are not clearly linked to an analysis of the learning needs of the students of the participating teachers. In other cases, leaders confuse provision for individual teacher career development with professional development, and the latter agenda is then dominated by activities that are not linked to student needs. In yet other cases, staff are given considerable discretion and support for pursuing innovations and new ideas, and it is a matter of chance rather than of design whether or not their individual projects improve teaching in ways that will raise student achievement in areas of need. If professional development is to be an effective engine for school improvement, then the development of teachers must serve the identified learning needs of students.

Focuses on the Relationship Between Teaching and Student Learning

Effective professional development involves intensive collaborative inquiry into the relationship between what has been taught and what students have learned. This type of linking talk is anchored in relevant evidence of students' work, whether it is in the form of standardized assessment results, project reports, artistic work, or essays. Skilled leadership is needed to help teachers link their accounts of their own teaching (resources used, activities planned, approaches taken, concepts explained) to its actual or possible impact on particular students. Similarly, skilled leadership is needed to guide teachers to link their discussion of students (home background, behavior in class, engagement with lesson) with features of the classroom environment and their own teaching. The proportion of time spent in such linking talk is higher in PLCs that make bigger shifts in student achievement, probably because there is a more intense focus on helping each other meet student learning goals (Timperley, 2005a).

Because the links between teaching and student learning are seldom obvious, the ladder of inference is an important leadership tool in helping teachers to test the validity of their inferences about these links. If a teacher claims, for example, that a child is not ready for a particular task, this claim can be checked through such questions as, "What observations lead you to believe he is not ready? What would convince you that he is ready? What other possibilities are there besides a lack of readiness?" Such leadership interventions increase teachers' awareness of the power of the assumptions they bring to their teaching and develop a culture of collaborative inquiry into their validity.

Provides Worthwhile Content

Effective professional development incorporates proven content. If the student need that drives the teacher learning is poor reading comprehension, then what content is being used to teach teachers how to improve comprehension? Is it a structured phonics approach, is it whole language teaching, or is it some combination of the two? What does the evidence say about the impact of the chosen approach? Leaders can increase the chance of getting worthwhile content by asking potential providers for any evaluations of their programs or by doing their own research on Web sites that provide robust syntheses of the evidence about the effectiveness of particular teaching approaches. The reports of the *Best Evidence Encyclopedia* out of Johns Hopkins University (www.bestevidence.org/) discussed in Chapter Four are an excellent resource on the relative effects of different approaches to teaching reading, math, and science at different year levels. Like all research-based generalizations, they are not an infallible guide to what might happen in any particular school, but they greatly increase the probability of making a wise investment of school or district money and teacher time.

Integrates Theory and Practice

Effective professional development integrates theoretical principles and practical applications. *Professional development by bullet point does not work* because it leaves teachers without the knowledge of underlying principles that enables them to create the conditions in their own classrooms that are the key to improved student learning. However, theoretical content that is not linked to practical applications and rich illustration is also ineffective. When teachers complain about content being too theoretical, they are not asking for less theory but for less theory that is disconnected from the classroom problems they are trying to solve. Effective professional development communicates clear theoretical principles and provides ample opportunity for participants to explore its practical implications for teaching in their own contexts.

Uses External Expertise

The use of external expertise is another feature of effective professional development. By external, I mean that the leadership of the PLC has demonstrated a greater capacity to solve or prevent the relevant teaching problems than the remaining group members. Expecting teachers who share similar difficulties to solve their problems without the help of such external expertise is unrealistic. The external expertise may be provided by another teacher in the same school, a coach, a researcher, or an external facilitator or consultant. The external expert needs, in addition to the capacity described previously, the ability to "challenge assumptions and present teachers with new possibilities; challenge the social norms by which collegial groups operate wherever these norms constrain professional learning; and keep the focus on students and their learning" (Timperley, 2008, p. 20).

The identification and authorization of in-school expertise may be a challenge in schools where it is assumed, at least publicly, that teachers are equally good at what they do. Challenges may also arise in teacher cultures in which the acceptance of influence is based on role, seniority, and experience rather than expertise. Formal leaders can challenge such cultures by treating expertise as task specific rather than generic, disclosing why they believe a particular teacher can be of assistance to his or her colleagues, and being open to teachers' feedback about their choices. Alternatively, teachers may choose their own experts, but steps should be taken to ensure that expertise rather than popularity is the basis for their choice.

Provides Multiple Opportunities to Learn

Like their students, teachers need multiple opportunities to learn, integrate, and apply new knowledge and skills. The evidence suggests that it is not the type of learning activities (discussion, readings, role-plays, coaching) that distinguishes effective professional development but the extent to which those activities are aligned to what it is that teachers are supposed to be learning. Close examination of the activities often shows that a considerable amount of time is taken up with activities that have little relevance to the practices that teachers are supposed to be learning. For example, too much time is taken up with "getting to know you" activities or brainstorming ideas about how to teach a topic rather than focusing in on the particular difficulties that teachers have or might experience. This reduces teachers' opportunities to learn, just as misaligned activities reduce students' opportunities to achieve intended learning outcomes (Chapter Five).

When professional development challenges teachers' existing practice and understandings, it may take one to two years for teachers to understand the difference between their current and the proposed practice, to develop the pedagogical content knowledge that supports the new practices, and, finally, to become comfortable with using them in their own classrooms. Decisions about how long to continue a particular type of professional development should be made by monitoring its impact on the target teaching practices and student outcomes. On the whole, professional development agendas are too ambitious for the allocated time, so the learning is fragmented, inadequately supported, and arbitrarily terminated when the money runs out. By contrast, however, some professional development is not terminated soon enough because unsubstantiated assumptions about the importance and effectiveness of the program are given more weight than credible site-based inquiry into the impact of the new instructional practice on student outcomes.

Skills for Leading Effective Professional Learning

Effective leadership of teacher professional learning is knowledgeable and skillful. When discussing this leadership dimension with school leaders, I am often asked for advice about what to do when teachers don't want to change. The question reflects the challenges leaders face in navigating the interpersonal and emotional dimensions of teacher professional learning. The following quote describes some of these interpersonal challenges.

> For PLCs to work teachers need to share ideas (even if they are criticized), share thoughts about instructional practices (even if proven that they do not work), and be open to hav[ing] the performance of their own students scrutinized by the members of the group or PLC (even if their own students are not performing very well). . . . So PLCs also are meant to be forums in which difficult conversations occur—conversations that must occur in order for the instructional practices of all

teachers to change and improve as the prime route to producing much higher levels of student learning. [Odden, 2009, p. 104]

In this section I build on my earlier discussion (Chapter Two) of open-to-learning conversations (OLCs) by explaining how the values and strategies that are central to such conversations are applied to the leadership of teacher change.

From Resistance to Theory Competition

We have all heard leaders describe particular teachers as "resistant to change." This is a common way of describing those who do not want to make the changes that their leaders advocate. Despite the fact that the change literature is replete with discussion about resistance and how to overcome it, I argue that the language of resistance is counterproductive to developing a teacher culture of collaborative continuous improvement. The language of resistance implies that the leaders are right and the resisters are wrong and thereby closes off the possibility of legitimate disagreement. Furthermore, the language of resistance deflects attention from the contribution of the change advocate to the teacher's reaction and thus treats the reaction as a personal fault rather than the possible result of the interaction between leader and teacher.

I advise leaders to abandon the language of resistance and reframe their teachers' reactions as the result of theoretical differences about the particular practices in question. The language of theory and theoretical difference takes the disagreement out of the realm of personality and into the much more impersonal realm of theory and theory evaluation. I should say at the outset that by "theory" I mean a theory of action—the values and beliefs that explain people's actions, together with the consequences of those actions. When we understand a person's theory of action we understand why he behaved as he did and we can work with him to evaluate whether or not the theory *in* his action matches his intentions (Argyris & Schön, 1996).

The following account of a leader's attempt to increase teachers' use of assessment data shows how the shift from the language of "resistance" to "theories of action" can help resolve disagreements about change. The context is an elementary school in which a new assistant principal was concerned that although teachers were regularly assessing their children's reading as required, they passed the results to their leaders without using them to make changes in their own reading program (Timperley, 2005b).

The assistant principal wanted the teachers to use the assessment data to plan reading lessons that would help their students make more rapid progress. She believed that by using the information on the various subtests, teachers would be able to tailor their lessons more precisely to their students' needs. She also believed that the teachers were not using the data because they did not understand or own them. After all, the data collection had been required by management rather than initiated by them. After due consideration, she decided to run a staff meeting to explain to teachers how useful the data could be. Despite her careful planning and leadership of the meeting, subsequent classroom observations and interviews with the teachers, conducted by an independent researcher, told her that nothing had changed. The teachers were still collecting but not using the assessment data.

The researcher's interviews were very revealing of the reasons why. The teachers sincerely believed that their students' low progress was due to factors beyond their control. They were already aware that their students were well below the required standard, and because there was little further they could do about it, what was the point of studying the data? Furthermore, they had doubts about the data's relevance and trustworthiness. Another reason they gave for not taking the data too seriously was that the standards were set unrealistically high for this type of school community. In short, although the assistant principal believed the data were useful, the teachers did not, and the result was "resistance to change."

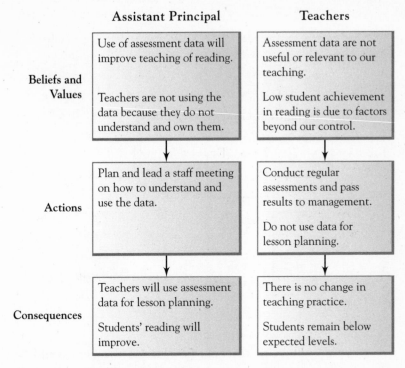

Figure 6.1   Two Competing Theories About the Use of Data
About Reading Achievement

In Figure 6.1, I reframe the teachers' resistance as a disagreement between two competing theories about the use of data. The theory of the assistant principal explains the actions she took to get the teachers to use the data. The theory of the teachers explains why they did not use it. Once we understand a person's theory of action we understand why she is not doing what we believe she ought to do. Her actions make sense because we understand the theory *in* her action.

Bypass and Engagement: Contrasting Approaches to the Leadership of Change

The mistake many leaders make when leading change is that they target the actions they want to change (limited use of data) without

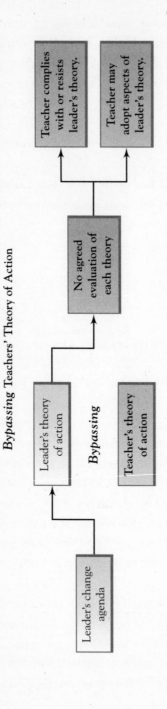

Bypassing Teachers' Theory of Action

Leader's change agenda → Leader's theory of action

Bypassing

Teacher's theory of action

Leader's theory of action → No agreed evaluation of each theory → Teacher complies with or resists leader's theory.

Teacher may adopt aspects of leader's theory.

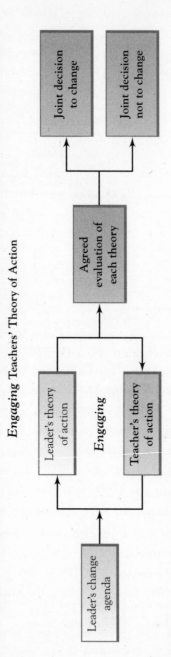

Engaging Teachers' Theory of Action

Leader's change agenda → Leader's theory of action

Engaging

Teacher's theory of action

Agreed evaluation of each theory → Joint decision to change

Joint decision not to change

Figure 6.2   Two Strategies for Leading Teacher Change

first understanding teachers' reasons for these actions. _In short, they don't ask enough questions of teachers about why they are doing what they want them to stop doing_. I call this the bypass strategy of change leadership because it ignores rather than engages the theory of action that explains the behavior the leader seeks to change (Figure 6.2). The assistant principal initially used a bypass strategy because she assumed rather than inquired into the reasons why the teachers were not using the assessment data. Her assumption that the teachers neither understood nor owned the data led to a conscientious and well-intentioned effort to persuade teachers of its usefulness. This effort was ultimately ineffective because it did not address the real reason why the teachers did not use the data, which was their belief that the low reading achievement was attributable to factors beyond their control (Figure 6.1).

Bypass and Engagement Strategies for Leading Change

In the bypass strategy it is the leader's theory that structures the conversation about change—usually consisting of reasons why an alternative approach is desirable. As shown in the upper portion of Figure 6.2, there is no connection between that theory and the theory of action of the persuasion target—hence the name _bypass strategy_. When disagreement is encountered, the typical response is to persuade harder. Convinced of the need to persuade the other to his or her own point of view, the leader remains closed to the possibility that the other person has sound reasons for preferring his or her current practice. The desire to win precludes the respect and genuine curiosity required to inquire into these reasons. For the leader, the consequence can be misdirected change strategies and frustration.

The target of change usually has a much better understanding of the thinking of the leader—after all, the teachers have been the target of his or her persuasion! What they struggle to understand is why the leader is not prepared to listen to their doubts, disagreements, and objections. The relationship deteriorates as the leader becomes increasingly frustrated with recalcitrant staff, and teachers become increasingly alienated from a leadership that fails to respect their point of view.

When there are large differences between theories of action, the bypass strategy will result in no agreement about the need to change. If the leader has the authority to force change, reluctant compliance will be the result. In the absence of such authority, the status quo will prevail. The bypass strategy is not always ineffective, however, because when the difference between the two theories is small, teachers will adjust their existing practice to incorporate compatible aspects of leaders' advice. Bypass is ineffective when more than minor adjustments are needed.

After learning from the researcher about the teachers' reasons for not using the data, the assistant principal switched to the engagement strategy portrayed in the lower section of Figure 6.2. She challenged the teachers' views that they had little control over the causes of low achievement by comparing the progress of their students on two different subtests. The results showed that although the students' ability to hear and record sounds now approached the required standard, their writing vocabulary was falling far behind. The teachers agreed that they had made a considerable difference to some aspects of their students' literacy. The assistant principal then led a discussion about why results on writing vocabulary were so low and whether different strategies might be more effective.

As the teachers tried new strategies for increasing writing vocabulary, some still expressed skepticism about whether the children were developmentally ready for such learning. The leader's response was to listen to and test teachers' reasoning by asking each teacher to track the children's vocabulary by having them write as many words as they could in five minutes. A month later, the assistant principal graphed the results, and the teachers discussed the progress each child had made. The graph showed large variation across the classes in the gains made in writing vocabulary.

The teachers were keen to identify and try the strategies used by the teacher whose children had made the most gains. Over a period of months, data use became a routine part of this meeting.

With the help of the external researcher, the assistant principal had shifted from a bypass to an engagement approach to change leadership. She now understood how the teachers were interpreting the change she was advocating (Spillane, Reiser, & Reimer, 2002), and that understanding changed her perception of the teachers from resistant to reasonable.

A Short Guide to Theory Engagement

Here is a short guide to leading change by engaging theories of action. Be forewarned, though—it will not work unless your leadership of change is informed by the open-to-learning values discussed in Chapter Two.

When you want people to change their current practice, do the following:

- State what your alternative practice is and why you believe it may be preferable to current practice.

- Listen to their reactions to your proposal.

- If the reaction is one of disagreement, inquire into the reasons for the disagreement. Usually this requires understanding the theory of action that sustains their current practice.

- Summarize your understanding of their current theory of action.

- Keep listening and summarizing until you are told by the other person that you have understood. This is the test of whether or not you have listened properly.

- Check that you both agree on the difference between the theory *in* the current practice and the theory in your proposed alternative.

- Collaborate on finding a way to test the implications and the importance of the difference.

- Keep testing and checking until you agree that change is not required or that a new theory of practice is worth trying.

It is important to note that the concept of engagement does not require leaders to personally inquire into the beliefs of everyone whom they wish to influence. If this were the case, the idea of theory engagement would have little purchase in the context of large schools, large-scale change, or policy development and implementation. Theory engagement requires deep understanding of the factors that sustain current practice and therefore of the challenges involved in changing it. There are many ways to gain such an understanding—through face-to-face dialogue with implementing agents, through pilot projects that focus on existing practice, or through study of relevant existing research. The principle at stake in all these change contexts—large or small—is that change advocates publicly test their understanding of the theories of action in which current practice is anchored. In this way they will come to understand the degree of match or mismatch between current theories of action and their proposed alternative. When leaders understand that match they understand the scope and depth of the change they are advocating.

Reflective Questions About Dimension Four Leadership

- To what extent is the research on the characteristics of effective professional learning used in the design and selection of teacher professional learning opportunities?

- To what extent does teacher collaborative learning focus on understanding the relationship between what has been taught and what students have learned?

- Is school professional development planning systematically linked to analysis of students' learning needs?

- To what extent are teachers' individual learning and develop-ment plans related to student learning needs?

- How effectively does the school identify teachers with the expertise needed to help colleagues address specific teaching problems?

- Is the impact on students used as an important indicator of the effectiveness of professional learning opportunities?

- To what extent do you employ bypass or engagement strategies in your leadership of change?

Summary

The most powerful leadership practices in terms of impact on student achievement are those included under Dimension Four, "Leading Teacher Learning and Development." They include creating high-quality collaborative opportunities for teachers to improve their teaching of what it is that their students are supposed to learn. Collaborative learning recognizes the interdependent nature of teachers' work, increases the coherence of the instruc-tional program, and makes more expertise and support available to individual teachers. The research evidence provides leaders with good guidance about the characteristics of professional learning that shift teaching in ways that advance the learning of students. Those characteristics include serving identified student and teacher learning needs, focusing on the relationship between teaching and student outcomes, providing worthwhile content, integrating theory and practice, using external expertise, and providing multiple opportunities to learn. The leadership capabilities introduced in Chapter Two were revisited in the context of leading teacher change. The values and skills of OLCs help leaders to reframe resistance to change as theoretical differences and to engage rather than bypass those differences. By investigating rather than dismissing teachers' reasons for their current practice, leaders will create the relationships they need to move from a unilateral to a more collaborative improvement agenda.

7

Dimension Five
Ensuring an Orderly and Safe Environment

From the point of view of leadership *action*, this dimension of leadership comes first. If students and staff do not feel physically and psychologically safe, if discipline codes are perceived as unfair and inconsistently enforced, then little progress is likely in the improvement of teaching and learning. When Mayor Michael Bloomberg took over control of New York City schools in 2002, the first stage of his two-part reform agenda was to bring order to their management, staffing, and organization. Once that was achieved, attention turned to achieving ambitious goals for improved teaching and learning (Odden, 2009). A similar sequence was followed in the reform of Chicago public schools (Bryk, Sebring, Kerbow, Rollow, & Easton, 1998).

The reason why this dimension is discussed last rather than first is that much of the knowledge leaders need to do this work well is embedded in the previous four dimensions and the three capabilities that underpin them. In the absence of order, educational improvement is unlikely, but, in acting to improve order, leaders must keep educational ends constantly kept in mind. If student management policies and procedures are disconnected from the quality of curriculum and instruction, the result is likely to be the increasing use of external incentives and sanctions to get students to engage in school and classroom activities from which they feel alienated. If, however, leaders understand such things as how students experience particular classes, how trust develops between teachers and students, and how good teaching fosters students' engagement and success, then student management policies and processes are more likely to serve educational values.

The Effect of Creating a Safe and Orderly Environment on Student Outcomes

Dimension Five was derived from eight studies that surveyed teachers about how their leaders performed tasks relevant to this dimension. The first aspect of this dimension concerns the orderliness and safety of the school's physical and social environment and includes practices such as the following:

- Providing a safe and orderly environment
- Providing a comfortable and caring environment
- Ensuring clear and consistently enforced discipline codes
- Ensuring high expectations for social behavior

The more positive the response of teachers on these survey items, the higher the achievement levels of the students, after differences in their background were taken into account (Heck, 2000; Heck, Marcoulides, & Lang, 1991).

A second aspect of this dimension involves protecting faculty from undue pressure from parents and officials (Heck, 1992; Heck, Marcoulides, & Lang, 1991). The leadership of high-performing schools was perceived by staff as more successful in this respect than the leadership of lower-performing schools serving a similar student body. This finding was particularly strong in high schools. Protection of this kind is not about being defensive—indeed, parent-school relationships, when assessed, were found to be more positive in high-performing schools. Rather, it is about allowing teachers to focus on their teaching while leaders mediate the messages that reach teachers from potentially disruptive lobby groups and parents.

A third aspect of Dimension Five involves conflict management. In one study, principal ability to identify and resolve conflict early, rather than allow it to fester, was strongly associated with student achievement (Eberts & Stone, 1986). The explanation may be that because effective conflict management builds trust in the school leadership, skilled conflict management increases leaders' ability to galvanize faculty around an improvement agenda. In schools where teachers and principals did not agree on the latter's conflict management skills, student academic performance was particularly low. This suggests wider problems of poor-quality feedback and communication between the principal and staff.

Across these studies, the average impact of this leadership dimension on student achievement was 0.27, suggesting that this type of leadership makes a small but important difference to the achievement of students. This effect is very similar to that which Marzano, Waters, and McNulty (2005) derived from their meta-analysis for this leadership dimension. Creating a safe and orderly environment is foundational in that although orderliness is not sufficient for a high-quality learning environment, its absence makes the work of educating students practically impossible.

A Student-Centered Perspective on Dimension Five

The purpose of Dimension Five leadership is to create a school environment that promotes the willing engagement of students in their own learning. Student engagement has three aspects: behavioral, emotional, and cognitive (Wang & Holcombe, 2010). Attendance at school, presence in class, and participation in extracurricular activities are indicators of behavioral engagement. Students who are emotionally engaged identify with their school and like at least some of their teachers, classes, and extracurricular activities. In Chapter Five, cognitive engagement was discussed in the context of a theory of effective teaching. Students who are thinking about the concepts and skills they are supposed to be learning are cognitively engaged. Such thinking includes self-regulatory strategies such as thinking about what is supposed to be learned, planning how to complete learning tasks, and checking their own work. In a safe and orderly environment these three types of student engagement will be high, and that engagement will be associated with strong student learning (Wang & Holcombe, 2010).

A holistic rather than narrow disciplinary approach is required. A singular focus on behavioral engagement, when students are not motivated to learn what is being offered, is punishing for both staff and students. Although students come to school with dispositions that shape their likelihood of engagement, there is an increasing body of evidence that students' perceptions of their schooling are an additional powerful determinant of how they engage with school. This evidence helps leaders to identify school norms and practices that lift or suppress levels of engagement. On the whole, student engagement is increased by school experiences that fulfill their psychological need for competence, autonomy, and relatedness (Deci & Ryan, 2000).

A sense of personal competence is fostered by student success in tasks and activities that are important to them. Learning opportunities that promote success involve well-structured activities that connect with students' prior experience and interests. Teachers also promote success by preventing repeated failure through their early detection and correction of students' misunderstandings (Chapter Five). Autonomy is promoted by school and class experiences in which students influence what and how they learn. This may involve making choices or, when choices are restricted, accepting the reasons teachers give them about why learning something is important (Absolum, 2006). A sense of autonomy is also fostered by teaching that enables students to regulate their own learning through knowledge of success criteria and of the progress they are making toward them. Relatedness is about affiliation and trust. When students feel that teachers know and care about them, they feel more connected to the school, and their emotional engagement provides a platform from which teachers can more readily foster their cognitive engagement with tough intellectual work.

Because there is considerable overlap between the patterns of school organization ánd school climate that foster these three types of engagement, they will be considered together in the remainder of the chapter. Two broad leadership strategies for increasing engagement are discussed: increasing students' sense of physical and psychological safety at school and in the classroom and increasing parent-school ties. The aim of both strategies is to foster students' engagement by meeting their need for competence, autonomy, and relatedness.

Increasing Engagement Through a Safe School Environment

The first step in increasing student engagement is to get students to school and in class. Although students' attendance reflects their health and what is happening at home, it is also responsive to what is happening at school. The importance of school-based explanations of attendance has been revealed by research showing that attendance rates vary widely across schools serving very similar communities and that these variations are partly explained by students' experience of the physical and psychological safety of the school environment (Bryk, Sebring, Allensworth, Luppescu, & Easton, 2010).

Leaders and teachers can test their assumptions about the safety of the school environment by asking students about their sense of security in hallways, in bathrooms, and on their way to and from school. Questions about bullying and intimidation can also be included in student surveys that give teachers valuable information about how students experience the school. School leaders who take such survey results seriously send strong signals to students about their commitment to creating a safe school and to judging safety by listening to students' voices.

Rates of school violence also vary widely between schools that serve very similar communities, suggesting that, as for school attendance, school culture and organization are important influences. A recent national study of violence in Israeli schools identified those schools whose rates of violence were atypical in the sense of being well above or well below what would be expected given the level of violence and deprivation in the communities they served (Astor, Benbenishty, & Estrada, 2009). The purpose of the study was to identify the factors within these atypical elementary, middle, and high schools that were responsible for the atypically high or low expressions of violence.

In the low-violence schools, principals mobilized staff around a vision of a peaceful school that was linked to a wider educational and political vision of how diverse communities could live together. Their vision was inspirational precisely because *it linked to community aspirations rather than community realities.* The goal was not just tighter discipline and better behavior but a school community that demonstrated its political and social values by the proactive pursuit of a peaceful and diverse society. The goal of a peaceful school was communicated to all members of the school community through appropriate cultural symbols, images, and text. Hallways included students' posters about peace and quotes from respected leaders and photos of members of different ethnic communities working together. Such communication was not seen as authentic, however, unless the symbolic messages were matched by school policy and practices. In many high-violence schools such symbols were seen as window dressing because they were not matched by consistent action.

Leaders in peaceful schools turned their vision into reality by working with staff to develop policies and procedures that were consistently carried out. These were not just about violence prevention and remediation. Values of inclusion and respect for diversity were evident every day in one Arab school where students and teachers learned sign language so they could communicate with a large group of deaf students. They were evident in another Jewish school in the spontaneous inclusion of students with cerebral palsy in the playtime games of their classmates. In high-violence schools, leaders addressed violent incidents through mass expulsions, heavy-handed searches, and intimidation. Although these tactics did succeed in reducing rates of severe violence, they also increased the sense of fear and intimidation. Management of violent incidents, in itself, does not increase students' sense of safety and security.

In peaceful schools, relationships were characterized by warmth and trust. Principals had a visible presence in hallways and courtyards, where they got to know and enjoy students personally. This was in stark contrast to the punitive or neglectful relationships found in high-violence schools. Caring for colleagues and students extended in peaceful schools to a whole-school responsibility for buildings and grounds. In peaceful schools, all staff took responsibility for violence-prone spaces and times, including local bus stops and playing fields. In high-violence schools, trash, dilapidated buildings and classrooms, and multiple security devices communicated neglect, threat, and lack of pride. Marginalized and disenfranchised students can experience such school environments as a sign of disrespect that reinforces their alienation from their school and its staff (Riley, 2007).

Principals played a central role in achieving safe schools through their work in galvanizing adults around an attractive vision, putting the routines in place to make the vision a reality, and building relational trust across the whole school community. Their role was far wider than is acknowledged in some evidence-based violence-prevention programs, where it is typically limited to ensuring faithful implementation of the program (Astor, Benbenishty, & Estrada, 2009).

Student safety and security within classrooms is promoted by teaching that ensures high-quality opportunities to learn

(Chapter Five). Students who are faced day after day with work that they neither understand nor relate to will eventually stay away from the classroom or be disruptive. Sometimes teachers respond to disruption and irregular attendance by reteaching old material, simplifying the work, and restricting learning activities to individual seat work. A vicious cycle develops of increased student boredom and passivity leading to increased absence and disruption, which teachers may respond to with more emphasis on practice drills and basic skills. Teachers need skilled help from instructional leaders to break this cycle of dysfunctional teacher-student interaction. When teachers offer active learning opportunities and more student choice, student attendance increases and classroom disruption decreases. "In general we know that children are more engaged in schooling when they feel in control of their own learning, are actively participating in the learning process, are interested in the topic being studied and are able to respond to the challenge before them. They are much less motivated by classes where they are cast in the role of passive recipients of knowledge to be delivered by the teacher" (Bryk, Sebring, Allensworth, Luppescu, & Easton, 2010, p. 104). In short, curriculum and pedagogy that recognize students' need for autonomy and competence increase engagement at school and in class.

Even in the most well-run classes, peers can pose threats to students' safety and well-being. For those students with low status in their peer group, peers can limit their access to the information and help they need to succeed in small-group activities. Without active teacher intervention, a partially hidden world of threats, name calling, obscenities, and racial abuse can thrive during group activities, even in classes in which behavioral engagement is high (Nuthall, 2007). Many instructional leaders, aware of this peer culture, ensure explicit teaching and enforcement of cooperative learning principles so that group activity supports the learning of all students.

Increasing Engagement Through Strong Parent-School Ties

Although the worlds of school and home may differ greatly, students will still thrive if there are enough bridges between them to make the crossing a walk into familiar rather than foreign territory. There are two sorts of bridges. One is built by leaders and teachers who know about, respect, and use the resources of the local community in their teaching and extracurricular activities. The other invites and supports parental involvement in the educational work of the school.

Both types of bridge build strong parent-school ties. Schools with strong ties tend to have safer school environments, better student attendance, and greater parent-school trust (Bryk, Sebring, Allensworth, Luppescu, & Easton, 2010; Epstein & Sheldon, 2002). These findings suggest that the leadership work of creating a safe and engaging school environment goes well beyond the school gate.

Building Ties Through the Curriculum

When we think about building stronger connections between home and school we tend to focus on how to inform and involve parents. But in this section I explain how such ties are also built by incorporating relevant aspects of student and community culture into their lessons. Although it is teachers who need to plan such lessons, leaders have an important role to play in ensuring, through their oversight of the curriculum, their analysis of student feedback, and their provision of teaching resources, that teachers are supported in making such connections. There are sound pedagogical reasons for linking classroom learning with students' lives:

> A *fundamental premise in instructional design is that one builds on the basic background knowledge, interests, and skills*

that students bring to the classroom. At the psychosocial level, a deep understanding of students' background represents a powerful resource for teachers as they seek to establish the interpersonal connections necessary to teach. At an instrumental level, good teachers draw on such background knowledge as they attempt to connect seemingly abstract academic topics to student lives. In this regard, knowing children well is essential to the effective design of classroom lessons that advance academic learning for all. [Bryk, Sebring, Allensworth, Luppescu, & Easton, 2010, p. 58]

In short, students are more motivated to learn if the lesson connects with their experience and interests. The connection makes the teacher more attractive and the material more comprehensible and relevant. The wider the gap between school and community cultures, the more important it is for teachers to make these connections.

Making those connections does not require every teacher to have direct contact with their students' families. This would be an impossible goal for high school teachers, who see up to 120 students per day. The key to making such connections in the classroom lies in well-designed units of work that connect academic concepts with relevant cultural ideas, skills, and activities. For example, when indigenous perspectives are integrated into quality learning tasks, the achievement of indigenous students can improve markedly. With the help of Yup'ik elders, teachers and researchers developed a series of culturally based mathematics curriculum modules for use in urban and rural Alaskan schools. Evaluations found that the Yup'ik students performed significantly better in the culturally based modules, particularly in terms of their understandings of mathematical concepts and their ability to transfer new knowledge to real-life situations (Lipka et al., 2005).

In large multicultural schools, there may be more than fifty different ethnic groups represented in the student body. Rather than expecting teachers to have curriculum-relevant knowledge about all such groups, it is more appropriate to focus on the attitudes and inquiry skills that enable teachers to learn, in context and as required, about how to make effective connections between the curriculum and cultural knowledge. It is the desire to make such connections and the provision of support for doing so that are important rather than the transmission of prepackaged information about students' cultures. Prepackaged information about "other cultural groups" or "other people's children" can contribute to stereotyped teacher views that impede the effective teaching of diverse students (Epstein, 2001). Rather than expecting teachers to be knowledgeable in the abstract about the cultures of their learners, the more appropriate expectation is that they learn enough about their students' lives to design learning activities, including homework tasks, that link academic concepts to culturally relevant practices (Mercado, 2001). The goal is that teachers and students become skilled at working between classroom and community cultures.

Building Ties Through Parental Involvement

There are many different ways of involving parents in their children's schooling, and on the whole, you reap what you sow. If leaders' efforts go into promoting parent involvement in the PTA or school governing body, then the consequences, assuming effective implementation, will be greater parental involvement in school events and school governance. There is little evidence of crossover effects—greater parental involvement in such activities does not typically lead to increased student achievement (Borman, Hewes, Overman, & Brown, 2003; Epstein, 2002). If the purpose of engaging the community is educational benefit for children, then leaders' efforts should go into involving parents in ways that create a stronger *educational* partnership between the school and its parents because that is the strategy that is most likely to deliver the intended results.

There is a complicating factor, however, and that is the issue of trust. Without trust building, all the parent evenings, newsletters, and cultural events in the world will yield disappointing results. Without trust building, leaders will not be able to break through the silence, defensiveness, face saving, or straight-out hostility that may have thwarted previous efforts to engage the parental community. If leaders have the knowledge and skills required to build trust they not only will achieve stronger community-school relationships but also will have created a social foundation from which parents and teachers can work together to improve students' engagement and achievement.

In Chapter Two, I introduced the idea of trust. It is worth reviewing it again in the context of what leaders can do to increase parents' trust of the school while seeking their greater involvement. Perhaps the most important thing to remember is that it is high-quality everyday interactions that build trust. Although participatory structures such as local school councils and special events may help, it is parents' judgments about how staff members treat them and their children that determine the level of trust.

In a study on parent-school trust conducted in seventy-nine midwestern elementary, middle, and high schools, parents expressed large differences in their average level of trust of their school (Adams, Forsyth, & Mitchell, 2009). The differences were not explained by the differing characteristics of the schools' communities but by factors internal to the schools' culture and organization. First, schools that gave parents genuine opportunities to influence school and classroom decisions were perceived as more trustworthy. These types of collaboration signal that the school respects parents' knowledge of their own children and is willing to be influenced by it. Parental influence came from multiple opportunities for parents and teachers to discuss educational issues rather than from structures, such as local school councils, which gave parents formal authority.

Second, greater parent trust was strongly associated with schools in which students themselves reported a strong sense of belonging to and valuing the school. When children agreed that "most of my teachers care about me" and "people in school are interested in what I have to say," their parents were much more likely to say that they trusted the school. This makes sense because children's reactions to school and their teachers are parents' most important source of information about the school. If their children feel cared for and like their teachers, parents are much more likely to trust the school. The clear implication for school leaders is that one way to increase parent-school trust is to ensure a positive relationship between teachers and students.

Although leaders do have considerable control over the conditions that promote trust, it is more easily achieved in some schools than others. It is easier in stable communities where parents and teachers can get to know one another and where parents have access to multiple sources of information about their school. It is harder in high schools where large size, subject-based teaching, and the increasing independence of children make it harder for teachers and parents to stay connected (Adams, Forsyth, & Mitchell, 2009).

Building trust in racially and culturally homogeneous communities is easier than in more diverse ones because people have a tendency to trust those they see as similar to themselves (Tschannen-Moran & Hoy, 2000). This is not a cause for guilt or blame but a reflection of the way social perception works. In more homogeneous communities and organizations, social similarities of race, ethnicity, and class provide grounds for an initial basis of trust and dissimilarities provide grounds for initial withholding of trust. This means that leaders of schools that serve culturally heterogeneous communities need to take more active steps to overcome mistrust. When parents are poor and teachers are seen as well off, when teachers are predominantly white and parents are predominantly Hispanic, more effort is required to grow trust. That effort should focus on improving the four qualities on which people make judgments of trustworthiness (Chapter Two).

When high trust is combined with effective strategies for parental involvement in their children's education, then student attendance and achievement are likely to increase.

Effective Strategies for Increasing Parental Involvement in Their Children's Education

The three quotes from elementary principals that follow tell something of the challenges of increasing parental involvement and of how to overcome them.

> *Principal: Real parental involvement in this school has been zilch. We have tried everything—reading mornings, maths mornings, free computer courses—some of these worked at first, but nothing really worked. They turn up for festivals and so on, but you can't get them involved in planning or curriculum sessions. [Benseman & Sutton, 2005, pp. 25–26]*
>
> *Principal: You know, I don't expect fifty parents to show up to a meeting about AYP because they don't care. But they do want to know about their child's reading ability and you know is my child doing well or is my child [not] doing well? . . . And let me say one thing about parent conferences. We pretty much get very close to 100 percent every time we have a parent conference. [Louis, Leithwood, Wahlstrom, & Anderson, 2010]*
>
> *Principal: So when I initially got here we had a PTA. We could never have a quorum. . . . I'm out and about and I talk to parents all the time. Why don't you come? Basically what we learned is they thought it was cliquish. So I wanted to dissolve the PTA and to dissolve a PTA you almost have to give them your first-born child. . . . Since I dissolved the PTA we use every last chair we've got for our meetings. It's whoever can help in whatever way is needed at any given time. So we have tremendous parental support in that regard. [Louis, Leithwood, Wahlstrom, & Anderson, 2010]*

The first principal is ready to give up—a lot of staff time, effort, and money have gone into strategies that have not worked—or at least not lasted. The second principal understands that the strongest motivation for parents' involvement is their own children, so that is her starting point for increasing her parents' involvement. The third principal understands that when things are not working, the key to finding out why is to ask parents themselves—not a select few but a wide range.

When repeated efforts to engage the community have not worked, one can understand why educators may blame the failure on parents. There is no doubt that some parent communities are harder to involve than others, but the level of involvement also reflects schools' strategies. Higher-quality programs attract more involvement, especially in interactive homework, volunteering, and school decision making (Sheldon & Van Voorhis, 2004). They also make an independent contribution to student achievement (Sheldon, 2003).

A sustained program of research out of Johns Hopkins University on the characteristics and development of effective home-school programs provides good guidance about what leaders can do to develop high-quality parent-involvement programs (Epstein & Jansorn, 2004; Sheldon, 2005).

- Develop a sustained and coherent program rather than a series of one-off initiatives. Plan to take about three years to develop a good program.

- Involve parents, teachers, and community leaders in oversight of the program so that the parties can share responsibility and be mutually accountable.

- Set goals that are linked to specific student needs, for example, improvements in aspects of student engagement and achievement.

- Embed the support of parental involvement in the school organization rather than contracting it out to specialist staff so that parents can learn from teachers and vice versa. It is strong parent-teacher and parent-leader relationships that increase trust and student engagement and achievement. If teachers are minimally involved, these relationships cannot develop.

- Work with community leaders and parents to locate resources that can help connect the curriculum to student and community cultures.

- Use evaluation data to progressively improve the program.

- Make regular substantive reports to the whole school community that acknowledge contributors and communicate the importance of this work, including its rationale, goals, and progress to date.

Schools use a wide range of strategies to involve their parents in their children's learning. At elementary school levels, these strategies often involve after-school workshops or meetings with a focus on a particular area of the curriculum. With careful planning, the effects of such workshops can be considerable. Design characteristics that appear to be important include making student learning the primary focus of the program, providing parents with explicit information and training (for example, modeling and reinforcing appropriate strategies for tutoring in reading), supplying materials for use at home, helping families access resources such as books, aligning school-home practices so that parents' actions support school learning, raising parents' expectations for their children's achievement, and using data on parent reactions and student progress to progressively improve the program.

At the high school level, involving parents in the academic guidance process, including providing early knowledge of curriculum pathways and their links to career choices, is, on average, more powerful than many other forms of involvement.

Most parents who are not currently involved in their children's schooling would like to be, but are unsure about how to help. Their hesitation is well founded because certain types of help can have counterproductive effects. If, for example, parents try to help with homework by supervising, checking up, and generally controlling their children, the result is likely to be a negligible or even negative impact on children's attitudes and achievement (Patall, Cooper, & Robinson, 2008). However, parental strategies that encourage study skills, such as setting clear homework rules and rewarding children accordingly, are more likely to be effective.

It seems clear that expecting parents to help with reading or with homework, without assessing parents' readiness to do so, is unlikely to work for either parents or students. Similarly, expecting teachers to engage parents in educational activities without attending to their learning needs is also likely to be ineffective. If teacher involvement is to be productive, they also need appropriate support and professional development. The aim of such development should be to increase teachers' knowledge of the school's communities, their confidence in communicating with diverse parents about their children's progress, and their ability to locate and integrate community resources into their teaching programs.

Reflective Questions About Dimension Five Leadership

- Are students surveyed regularly about their attitudes toward the school and their learning?

- How thoroughly are the results of such surveys used for the purpose of improvement?

- Are student management policies explicitly linked to broader social values about a well-functioning community?

- How well does school leadership support teachers in using relevant community resources in their teaching?

- To what extent are parent-involvement efforts focused on increasing parental engagement with the educational work of the school?

- To what extent does school leadership coordinate and monitor the effectiveness of parent-involvement efforts?

Summary

Viewed from an educational rather than a managerial perspective, the work of creating a safe and orderly school is fundamentally about increasing the physical, emotional, and cognitive engagement of students by meeting their needs for caring relationships and for control over and success in their learning. Students' engagement with school, particularly their attendance, is strongly affected by whether they judge it to be physically and psychologically safe and whether they feel that most of their teachers care about them. It is also affected by the strength of parent-school ties. Strong ties are made by linking teaching programs with relevant community resources and by educationally focused parent involvement. Leaders play a central role in orchestrating a coherent and evidence-based approach to parent involvement and in building the trust that enables parents and teachers to work together to increase the engagement of all students.

8

Putting Education Back into Educational Leadership

Although we have always known that the quality of leadership makes a difference to the working lives of teachers, it has been harder to discern how it affects the success of *students*. Part of the difficulty was that we were asking the wrong question. It is not particularly fruitful to ask whether *leaders* make a difference to student learning or achievement because the answer depends on what it is that they *actually do*. Indeed, the most defensible answer to that question is probably that school leaders, on the whole, don't make much difference to their students' achievement (O'Shaughnessy, 2007). A better question is, "What types of *leadership practice* make a difference?" We now know quite a lot about what those practices are and which capabilities leaders require to perform them competently.

The five dimensions and three capabilities of student-centered leadership described and explained in this book provide a detailed, evidence-based picture of how leaders make an educational difference to the learning and achievement of their students. First, student-centered leadership involves the determined pursuit of clear goals, which are linked to important educational and social purposes. Goal setting (Dimension One) is a powerful leadership tool in the quest for improving learning and teaching because it signals to staff which things are more important than others. Clear learning goals, together with the associated organizational routines, ensure that staff effort and attention are focused on reducing the gap between aspiration and reality. Without clear goals, staff effort is dissipated in multiple agendas and conflicting priorities, which over time can produce burnout, cynicism, and disengagement.

Because considerably more happens in schools than the pursuit of explicit goals, even the most goal-focused leaders need to skillfully manage the constant distractions that threaten to undermine their best intentions. Such distractions, in the form of new policy initiatives, school crises, calls for goal revision or abandonment, and the need to maintain school routines that are not directly goal related, all threaten to undermine goal pursuit (Levin, 2008). Clear goals enable leaders to recognize that they are being distracted and to decide what to do about it.

Clarity around educational goals makes strategic resourcing possible (Dimension Two). The challenge of Dimension Two leadership is the allocation and reallocation of existing resources in light of the schools' own priorities and the evidence about how they can be met. There are tight connections between Dimension Two leadership and the three capabilities of effective leadership. The ability to challenge assumptions about how to resource the work of the school, to deal with the emotional fallout of reallocation while listening carefully to all the objections, to select "smart" rather than "dumb" instructional tools, to find the degrees of freedom needed to change a schedule—all these leadership activities require the ability to integrate educational knowledge, relationships, and problem solving. Without deep knowledge, leaders can select instructional tools that shape teachers' practices in ways that do not serve instructional goals; without a foundation of trust they can make evidence-based allocation decisions but still damage the relationships they need to make those decisions drive the improvement they seek. Dimension Two leadership, as for all five dimensions, requires a skillful integration of the "what" and the "how" of leadership.

Ensuring the quality of teaching (Dimension Three) is at the heart of instructional leadership. In high schools, much of this leadership would be carried out by subject specialists such as department chairs and curriculum leaders, and the principal would be best described as the leader of instructional leaders. Increasing the impact of Dimension Three leadership is not simply a matter of mandating more classroom visits, teacher observations, or more discussion of teaching and learning at staff meetings. More classroom visits and teacher feedback could make matters worse if the feedback were based on a faulty theory of teaching quality. If leaders use closed rather than open-to-learning approaches to feedback, the results could be little learning and reduced trust.

Once again, we see the necessity of leadership building relationships of trust *while* doing the work of improving teaching and learning. For some leaders, simultaneous attention to task and relationships runs counter to what I affectionately call their "cup of coffee" theory of leadership. (In Australia I call it the "have a few beers" theory of leadership.) In this theory, relationships with staff are developed through socializing together, and only when a certain level of mutual comfort is developed are higher-stakes tasks and topics introduced. One problem with this approach is that trust is built by demonstrating respect, integrity, and competence (Chapter Two). Low-risk socializing provides very limited opportunities for demonstrating these qualities, so it is unlikely to build the anticipated platform of trust. A second problem is that although the adults are getting comfortable with one another, the higher-risk discussion, which is often about teacher performance, has been postponed. This means that the interests of students have been sacrificed for the comfort of the adults. A better approach is to tackle the issue, when it arises, through an open-to-learning conversation that progresses the problem *and* builds the relationship.

Arguably, direct involvement in teacher professional learning (Dimension Four) is the most powerful way that leaders can influence the quality of teaching and learning in their school. Its goal is to develop the capacity of teachers to teach what students need to learn while being open minded about what that is and how to achieve it. It has a strong focus on collaborative analysis of the relationship between what students have learned and how they have been taught. Much of this work should be collaborative because it is hard work, because relevant expertise is not found in the head of one person, and because systematic collaborative learning builds a professional practice that reduces the isolation of teachers and the variation in teaching quality.

It would be easy to criticize my emphases on instructional program coherence (Dimension Three), collaborative learning, and collective responsibility (Dimension Four) as promoting a one-size-fits-all type of teaching and teacher learning. Although we can all readily agree that feet of widely varying shapes should not be shoved into the same ill-fitting shoe, too often the analogy from clothing is used as an intellectually lazy way of defending idiosyncratic teaching. Induction into a shared professional practice does not preclude professional judgment. To take just one example, theories of learning tell us that children learn and remember new ideas when they can link those ideas to what they already know (Nuthall, 2000). These theories of learning are linked to theories of teaching that tell us that teachers need to find out what children already know and design learning activities that connect with and extend their prior knowledge (Chapter Five). All teachers need to know how to make these connections, and, in this sense, one size *does* fit all. There is still wide scope for professional judgment, because teachers need to tailor their lessons and resources to suit the differing prior knowledge of their students. Standard professional practice provides the scaffolding for the exercise of truly professional rather than idiosyncratic judgment.

Student-centered leadership reaches beyond the school gates to parents and the wider community. The work of ensuring an orderly and safe environment (Dimension Five) is enhanced by strong parent-school ties born of a deep respect for the aspirations that parents have for their children and an empathy for the conditions under which they may be trying to realize them.

Strong ties are developed by bringing relevant cultural resources into the school and classrooms and by more direct involvement of parents in the educational work of the school.

The evidence I presented in Chapter One about the *average* relative impact of these five dimensions on student achievement should not be interpreted as meaning, for example, that the leadership of any given school should give twice as much emphasis to the leadership of teacher learning and development as it does to ensuring an orderly and safe environment. Schools at different stages of development will need different emphases. In schools where teachers and students struggle to get to class on time, a focus on orderliness, safety, and civility may be an essential prior stage before leaders can give more attention to teacher learning and development. The evidence does mean, however, that the school leadership is likely to have an even bigger impact on student achievement when it can focus more directly on the quality of learning, teaching, and teacher learning.

Throughout this book my emphasis has been on using the evidence about leadership impact to inform context-specific decisions about how and what to lead. There are no leadership rules and there never will be because the contextual complexity involved in every leadership decision precludes them. When an Australian district leader instructed all his principals to attend a two-day professional development event with their teachers and justified it by appealing to "Viviane's findings" about the impact of Dimension Five leadership, I was forced to reflect on how I had contributed to this rule-based approach. Why had he focused on the impact of Dimension Five rather than on my explanation of its power? If he had understood the explanation, rather than requiring attendance, he would have checked what his principals already knew about the new practices and the conditions their teachers needed to make them work in their classrooms.

The three capabilities are important precisely because the five dimensions are not rules. Figuring out how the dimensions work in particular contexts requires skill in using educational and situational knowledge to engage in repeated cycles of problem solving about how to improve teaching and learning. Trust provides the social foundation that makes this collective work both possible and deeply satisfying.

There is a paradox in expecting leaders to have a clear focus in the highly fragmented world of educational policy and practice. And yet nothing of importance is achieved in schools without sustained, collective, and focused effort. Although I addressed many of the challenges of maintaining focus in my discussion of goal setting (Chapter Three), problem solving is also highly relevant because it requires the ability to integrate widely disparate elements. In my discussion of problem solving (Chapter Two), I described this as a process of discerning, evaluating, and crafting a solution that, *as far as possible*, integrates all the important solution requirements. The leadership skill is in synthesizing the competing tendencies—going beyond the fragments to see the unifying possibilities. This is an especially difficult challenge for those leaders who notice conflicts, tensions, and competing forces much more readily than their integrative possibilities. It is even more difficult if each of the competing forces has attracted its own lobby group. But the research on expert problem solving tells us that this integrative skill can be learned. And the values of respect and inclusion associated with OLCs show how to involve others in the search for the integrative thread. So part of the answer to the question of how to keep focus in a fragmented world is to create it, by ignoring what you can, creatively transforming what is of use, and constantly reading the world through the lens of your educational goals.

Student-Centered Leadership Requires Educational Expertise

In most educational jurisdictions there has been a major shift in the focus of school accountability policies from accountability for inputs (for example, money spent, quality of teaching staff, resource allocation) and compliance with regulations to account-ability for reaching specified levels of student performance (Elmore, 2004).

The new focus on results and the increased accountability of school leaders for achieving them have transformed the role of the principal. Previously, the principal was expected to be an effec-tive manager—the person who ensured compliance with a host of regulations and looked after parents, property, finances, and stu-dent discipline. Now, the expectation is that school leaders can work positively with their teachers to improve instruction. Here is how one Texas middle school leader expressed the effect of new accountability policies on his role:

> Before state accountability came in it was sort of a hit and miss situation. It was just, it was more that the principal was more of a manager. I mean I kept the keys, I opened the building, I closed the building. And now I see the transition where the principal is no longer, well, he's still that to a cer-tain extent, but now he's more the instructional leader of the campus where he's held accountable for instruction and for the learning that is taking place. In the years past you could judge a principal by basically is his building clean? Are his kids behaving? And if the answer is yes it didn't really matter whether they were scoring high or scoring low. Nowadays that is not the case. [Skrla, Scheurich, & Johnson, 2000, p. 33]

Although the accountability policies have created new expec-tations, they do not, in themselves, create the capacity to meet them. One of the major messages of this book is that if leaders are to achieve the expected results, they need access to up-to-date knowledge about teaching and learning and skill in using that knowledge to shape educationally sound administrative practices. Knowing about the five dimensions of student-centered leadership is not enough—leaders also need to understand their underlying principles so they can discriminate between education-ally sound and unsound homework policies, teacher evaluation policies and procedures, instructional frameworks, student support strategies, and professional development activities. The scope and depth of the knowledge required are too great for any one leader or leadership team to master—specialization and networked learn-ing opportunities are essential. So, too, are smart tools—well designed and knowledge rich—that scaffold the practice and the learning of school leaders in ways that substantially increase their chance of achieving their goals (Chapter Four).

The title of this chapter comes from an article in which I argued that educational leadership research and practice needed to be more strongly anchored in knowledge of teaching and learn-ing (Robinson, 2006). Although the argument resonated with many of my readers who were frustrated with the managerial emphasis of their role, others objected that education did not have to be "put back" into educational leadership because it had never been "taken out." Their classroom teaching experience had given them the educational expertise. What they needed now, they asserted, was to learn how to be leaders, and that meant attending business courses and reading the type of motivational books found in the management section of airport bookshops.

I do not want to reject the usefulness of generic management skills but I do want to shift the balance toward greater emphasis on the knowledge and skills that are specific to educational lead-ership. The issue turns, for me, not on one's attitudes to business or educational knowledge, but on the evidence about what leaders need to know and be able to do to make a bigger educational difference for their students. If management theory and skills are useful for these purposes then let us use them, but let us also recognize their limits. Although aspiring and current school leaders may learn something useful about personnel evaluation from an MBA course, such courses will not teach them about the validity of the theory of effective teaching that is implicit in their evaluation tools. Making the link between the business course and their educational context is not just a matter of *applying* their business knowledge because that assumes that what they have learned is applicable. If, for example, the only evaluation tools they have been exposed to are behavioral checklists, this knowledge is probably not applicable to the evaluation of teaching (Chapter Five). Leaders' educational knowledge must be strong enough to transform generic knowledge in ways that clearly serve educational ends.

Throughout the book I have provided examples of how educational leaders and policy makers underestimate the capacity— both knowledge and skills—that teachers need to meet society's ambitious expectations of schools. I am repeatedly struck when working with either group by how quick they are to assume that when goals are not met or policies are not properly implemented the problems are caused by teachers' lack of will rather than skill. I see leaders who are frustrated by the poor practices of a teacher persistently asking that same teacher for ideas about how they could improve. Such leaders are often surprised when I ask them why they assume that teachers who are struggling really know how to solve their difficulties. If they knew what to do differently, wouldn't they have already done it?

The will rather than skill explanation is symptomatic of the trivialization of educational expertise. In City, Elmore, Fiarman, and Teitel's (2009) book on instructional rounds, the authors write, "the nineteenth century idea that teaching is relatively low skill work that can be performed by anyone with a nodding familiarity with content and an affinity for children is alive and well in the policy discourse of the present reform period. . . . Presently, policy makers and critics lack much understanding of the actual knowledge and skill requirements of what they are asking educators to do" (pp. 11–12).

If my argument about the importance of integrating deep knowledge of teaching and learning into administrative practice is correct, then schools should be led by educators rather than by generic managers. Although there is an important place for business expertise within the knowledge mix of a leadership team, the balance should be in favor of educational expertise because *leading the work requires deep knowledge of the work*.

Value and Enjoy Leadership

Although there are many stories about leaders who abuse their power, there are far fewer about leaders who fail because of their unwillingness to exercise it. Yet in my experience, reluctance to exercise influence is an equally important cause of leadership ineffectiveness. In the culture of teaching, powerful norms about democracy, professional autonomy, and collegiality contribute to a deep ambivalence about the exercise of leadership. People fear standing out from their peers, being called *bossy* or *know it all* or being disrespectful of those with more seniority or experience than themselves. Such norms reinforce a culture of niceness that inhibits leadership and the critical collegial talk that is essential to a well-functioning professional learning community. Facilitators involved in the instructional rounds approach to professional learning characterize this "land of nice" culture as, "If you haven't got anything nice to say, don't say anything at all" (City, Elmore, Fiarman, & Teitel, 2009, p. 76). If we are going to substantially increase the frequency and quality of the leadership practices described by the five dimensions, then we need all educators to feel comfortable exercising the fluid and task-specific type of leadership I described in the opening chapter of this book. If we don't change these norms so that more educators are comfortable attempting to influence their colleagues, whether or not they hold leadership positions, then our talk about distributed leadership is just that—talk.

Table 8.1 illustrates the problem of ambivalent leadership. The context is a literacy leader working with her colleagues to

Table 8.1. Ambivalent Leadership of a Team Meeting

Leader's Words	Interpretation of Leader's Words
"I just wanted to just . . ."	Language is tentative.
"Very quickly go through the latest bit of data"	This may not deserve much time.
"If you don't want it just give it back to me . . ."	Serious engagement with the data is voluntary.
"I know it's a paper war . . ."	The data represent yet another piece of paper.
"You don't have to file it or anything like that at this stage . . . it's just handwritten."	This piece of paper may not be important.

examine the reading progress of their Year 1 students (Timperley et al., 2004). On the left-hand side are excerpts from the meeting transcript that show how she introduced the record of students' achievement. On the right-hand side are my own interpretations of her messages.

The leader acts as if she has not accepted that she *is* the leader of the group and that providing direction is part of her role. Perhaps her tentativeness reflects her concern about whether or not her direction will be accepted. The solution to ambivalence about the exercise of influence is not to minimize or otherwise disguise one's leadership attempts. Switching from this soft-sell approach to a more hard-sell approach is not the answer either. An open-to-learning approach requires a clear declaration of one's agenda and inquiry into others' reactions and points of view.

The skills and values of an OLC support confident rather than ambivalent leadership because they encourage clear disclosure of one's point of view together with openness to others' reactions. The literacy leader can overcome her ambivalence by stating clearly what she wants the team to do and why, and asking for their reaction. If she could do that she would probably enjoy her leadership more.

Although ambivalence about the exercise of influence reduces the enjoyment of leadership, conviction about its importance, combined with the capability to do it well most of the time, increase enjoyment. Making a difference to thirty students in their own class satisfies and sustains teachers. Making a difference to nearly all the students in a school satisfies and sustains educational leaders.

My message about the impact of the five dimensions does not deny that there are limits to the impact leaders can have on student achievement. We know that the home background of students shapes how they perform at school and that the poverty and deprivation of some communities pose formidable obstacles to classroom learning. We also know, however, that school-based influences on teacher recruitment, teacher retention, student attendance, students' sense of safety, student achievement, parent involvement, and parent-school trust are a lot bigger than is often assumed. We *discover rather than declare* the limits of school leaders' influence by continual inquiry into the conditions and capabilities that enable them to be more effective. This also applies to the research findings that form the core evidence of this book (Figure 1.1). There is no reason why the size of leadership effects could not be even larger in school systems that focus on the five leadership dimensions and systematically develop the three capabilities that underpin them.

Leadership or Management?

Academics sweat blood over making conceptual distinctions between leading and managing. Practitioners and academics make status distinctions between them, with leaders trumping managers on the status hierarchy. Apparently, leaders determine the right thing to do, and managers follow their lead by doing the right thing the right way (Mintzberg, 2009). I am inclined to agree with Mintzberg's (2009) reflection on this distinction:

"Frankly, I don't understand what the distinction means in the everyday life of organizations. Sure, we can separate leading and managing conceptually. But can we separate them in practice? Or, more to the point, should we even try?" (p. 8).

In the first chapter of this book I described leadership as an influence process in which the source of the influence is others' acceptance of the reasonableness of the influence attempt or respect of the leader as a person. Without that acceptance or identification, there is no influence and no exercise of leadership. Because managers, by definition, are responsible for other staff, surely they must be able to lead as well? And how do leaders know what the "right" things are if they don't deeply understand aspects of the business they are in? If leaders confine themselves to the "big picture," they are likely to paint one that bears little connection to what is on the ground and, worse still, not know that this is what they have done.

Leadership requires the constant integration of the detail and the big picture so that policy is connected to practice and learns from its implementation, so that goals are realistic and achievable, so that action informs planning as well as vice versa. Although leaders can fall into the trap of micromanaging and never get to formulate a big picture, they can also fail by macroleading—exercising authority without sufficient knowledge of the detail and sufficient appreciation of the implications of the big picture for the troops on the ground. Once again, the way through is integration—to see the considerable overlap between leading and managing and the necessity of both being strongly anchored in the educational work. As I said at the outset of this book, most educators share the ambition of having all children succeed at school. What we need to get better at is developing and supporting leaders who can lead and manage in ways that make that vision a reality in single schools, in school networks, and in whole systems. Achieving the vision requires their work to be deeply informed by knowledge of how to improve learning and teaching. That is why we must put education back into educational leadership.

References

Absolum, M. (2006). *Clarity in the classroom*. Auckland, NZ: Hodder Education.

Adams, C. M., Forsyth, P. B., & Mitchell, R. M. (2009). The formation of parent-school trust: A multilevel analysis. *Educational Administration Quarterly, 45*(1), 4–33.

Aitken, G. (2005). *Curriculum design in New Zealand social studies: Learning from the past* (Doctoral thesis). University of Auckland, NZ.

Alig-Mielcarek, J. M., & Hoy, W. K. (2005). Instructional leadership: Its nature, meaning, and influence. In C. G. Miskel & W. K. Hoy (Eds.), *Educational leadership and reform* (pp. 29–52). Greenwich, CT: Information Age Publishing.

Andrews, R., & Soder, R. (1987). Principal leadership and student achievement. *Educational Leadership, 44*(6), 9–11.

Argyris, C. (1991). Teaching smart people how to learn. *Harvard Business Review, 69*(3), 99–109.

Argyris, C. (1993). Education for leading learning. *Organizational Dynamics, 21*(3), 5–17.

Argyris, C., & Schön, D. (1974). *Theory in practice: Increasing professional effectiveness*. San Francisco: Jossey-Bass.

Argyris, C., & Schön, D. A. (1996). *Organizational learning II: Theory, method and practice*. Reading, MA: Addison Wesley.

Astor, R. A., Benbenishty, R., & Estrada, J. N. (2009). School violence and theoretically atypical schools: The principal's centrality in orchestrating safe schools. *American Educational Research Journal, 46*(2), 423–461.

Bamburg, J. D., & Andrews, R. L. (1991). School goals, principals and achievement. *School Effectiveness & School Improvement, 2*(3), 175–191.

Barnett, K., McCormick, J., & Conners, R. (2001). Transformational leadership in schools: Panacea, placebo or problem? *Journal of Educational Administration, 39*(1), 24–46.

Benseman, J., & Sutton, A. (2005). *Summative evaluation of the Manukau Family Literacy Project (2004)*. Wellington, NZ: City of Manukau Education Trust (COMET).

Berliner, D. (1987). Simple views of effective teaching and a simple theory of classroom instruction. In D. Berliner & B. Rosenshine (Eds.), *Talks to teachers*. New York: Random House.

Berliner, D. (1990). What's all the fuss about instructional time? Retrieved from http://courses.ed.asu.edu/berliner/readings/fuss/fuss.htm.

Blatchford, P., Bassett, P., Brown, P., Martin, C., Russell, A., & Webster, R. (2010). *The impact of teacher aides/assistants on pupils' "positive approaches to learning" and their academic progress*. Paper presented at the Annual Meeting of the American Educational Research Association, Denver, CO.

Borman, G., Hewes, G. M., Overman, L. T., & Brown, S. (2003). Comprehensive school reform and achievement: A meta-analysis. *Review of Educational Research, 73*(2), 125–230.

Bransford, J. D., Brown, A. L., & Cocking, R. R. (Eds.). (2000). *How people learn: Brain, mind, experience, and school* (Expanded ed.). Washington, DC: National Academy Press.

Bridges, E. M. (1986). *The incompetent teacher*. Lewes, UK: Falmer Press.

Bryk, A. S., & Schneider, B. L. (2002). *Trust in schools: A core resource for improvement*. New York: Russell Sage Foundation.

Bryk, A. S., Sebring, P. B., Allensworth, E., Luppescu, S., & Easton, J. Q. (2010). *Organizing schools for improvement*. Chicago: University of Chicago Press.

Bryk, A. S., Sebring, P. B., Kerbow, D., Rollow, S., & Easton, J. Q. (1998). *Charting Chicago school reform: Democratic localism as a lever for change*. Boulder, CO: Westview Press.

Cardno, C. (2007). Leadership learning—The praxis of dilemma management. *International Studies in Educational Administration, 35*(2), 33–50.

City, E., Elmore, R. F., Fiarman, S., & Teitel, L. (2009). *Instructional rounds in education*. Cambridge, MA: Harvard Education Press.

Cooper, H., Nye, B., Charlton, K., Lindsay, J., & Greathouse, S. (1996). The effects of summer vacation on achievement test scores: A narrative and meta-analytic review. *Review of Educational Research, 66*(3), 227–268.

Council of Chief State School Officers. (2008). *Educational leadership policy standards: ISLLC 2008*. Washington, DC: Author.

Cuban, L. (2008). The perennial reform: Fixing school time. *Phi Delta Kappan, 90*(4), 240–250.

Darling-Hammond, L. (2006). Securing the right to learn: Policy and practice for powerful teaching and learning. *Educational Researcher, 35*(7), 13–24.

Deci, E. L., & Ryan, R. M. (2000). The "what" and "why" of goal pursuits: Human needs and the self-determination of behavior. *Psychological Inquiry, 11*(4), 227–268.

Department for Children, Schools and Families. (2009). *Statistical first release: School workforce in England (including pupil: teacher ratios and pupil: adult ratios), January 2009 (provisional).* (SFR 09/2009). London: Author.

Earl, L., & Fullan, M. (2003). Using data in leadership for learning. *Cambridge Journal of Education, 33,* 383–394.

Earl, L., & Katz, S. (2002). Leading schools in a data-rich world. In K. Leithwood & P. Hallinger (Eds.), *Second international handbook of leadership and administration* (pp. 1003–1022). Dordrecht, Germany: Kluwer Academic.

Eberts, R. W., & Stone, J. A. (1986). Student achievement in public schools: Do principals make a difference? *Economics of Education Review, 7*(3), 291–299.

Elmore, R. F. (2004). *School reform from the inside out: Policy, practice, and performance.* Cambridge, MA: Harvard Education Press.

Elmore, R., & Burney, D. (1999). Investing in teacher learning: Staff development and instructional improvement. In L. Darling-Hammond & G. Sykes (Eds.), *Teaching as the learning profession* (pp. 263–291). San Francisco: Jossey-Bass.

Epstein, J. L. (2001). *School, family and community partnerships: Preparing educators and improving schools.* Boulder, CO: Westview Press.

Epstein, J. L. (2002). School/family/community partnerships: Caring for the children we share. In J. Epstein, M. G. Sanders, B. Simon, K. Salinas, N. Jansorn, & F.L.V. Voorhis (Eds.), *School, family, and community partnerships: Your action handbook* (2nd ed., pp. 7–29). Thousand Oaks, CA: Corwin Press.

Epstein, J. L., & Jansorn, N. R. (2004). Developing successful partnership programs: Principal leadership makes a difference. *Principal, 83,* 10–15.

Epstein, J. L., & Sheldon, S. (2002). Present and accounted for: Improving student attendance through family and community involvement. *Journal of Educational Research, 95*(5), 308–318.

Friedkin, N. E., & Slater, M. R. (1994). School leadership and performance: A social network approach. *Sociology of Education, 67*(2), 139–157.

Fullan, M. G. (1992). Visions that blind. *Educational Leadership, 49*(5), 19–22.

Gerber, S. B., Finn, J. D., Achilles, C. M., & Boyd-Zaharias, J. (2001). Teacher aides and students' academic achievement. *Educational Evaluation and Policy Analysis, 23*(2), 123–143.

Goddard, R. D., Hoy, W. K., & Hoy, A. (2000). Collective teacher efficacy: Its meaning, measure, and impact on student achievement. *American Educational Research Journal, 37*(2), 479–507.

Gordon, E. E. (2009). 5 ways to improve tutoring programs. *Phi Delta Kappan, 90*(6), 440–445.

Hallinger, P. (2005). Instructional leadership and the school principal: A passing fancy that refuses to fade away. *Leadership and Policy in Schools, 4*(3), 221–239.

Hallinger, P., & Heck, R. H. (1998). Exploring the principal's contribution to school effectiveness: 1980–1995. *School Effectiveness and School Improvement, 9*(2), 157–191.

Hargreaves, A., & Fink, D. (2006). *Sustainable leadership.* San Francisco: Jossey-Bass.

Hart, W., Albarracin, D., Eagly, A., Brechan, I., Lindberg, M. J., & Merrill, L. (2009). Feeling validated versus being correct: A meta-analysis of selective exposure of information. *Psychological Bulletin, 135*(4), 555–588.

Hattie, J. (2009). *Visible learning: A synthesis of over 800 meta-analyses relating to achievement.* London: Routledge.

Heck, R. H. (1992). Principals' instructional leadership and school performance: Implications for policy development. *Educational Evaluation and Policy Analysis, 14*(1), 21–34.

Heck, R. H. (2000). Examining the impact of school quality on school outcomes and improvement: A value-added approach. *Educational Administration Quarterly, 36*(4), 513–552.

Heck, R. H., Larsen, T. J., & Marcoulides, G. A. (1990). Instructional leadership and school achievement: Validation of a causal model. *Educational Administration Quarterly, 26*(2), 94–125.

Heck, R. H., Marcoulides, G. A., & Lang, P. (1991). Principal instructional leadership and school achievement: The application of discriminant techniques. *School Effectiveness and School Improvement, 2*(2), 115–135.

Hess, F. M. (1999). *Spinning wheels: The politics of urban school reform.* Washington, DC: The Brookings Institution.

Horn, I. S., & Little, J. W. (2010). Attending to problems of practice: Routines and resources for professional learning in teachers' workplace interactions. *American Educational Research Journal, 47*(1), 181–217.

Ingersoll, R. M. (2001). Teacher turnover and teacher shortages: An organizational analysis. *American Educational Research Journal, 38*(3), 499–534.

Konstantopoulos, S., & Chung, V. (2010). The persistence of teacher effects in elementary grades. *American Educational Research Journal.* Advance online publication. doi:10.3102/0002831210382888.

Kruse, S., Louis, K. S., & Bryk, A. (1994). Building professional communities in schools. In *Issues in restructuring schools* (Issue Report no. 6, pp. 3–6). Madison: Center on Organization and Restructuring of Schools, University of Wisconsin. Retrieved from www.wcer.wisc.edu/archive/cors/Issues_in_Restructuring_Schools/ISSUES_NO_6_SPRING_1994.pdf.

Latham, G. P., & Locke, E. A. (2006). Enhancing the benefits and overcoming the pitfalls of goal setting. *Organizational Dynamics, 35*(4), 332–340.

Latham, G. P., & Locke, E. A. (2007). New developments and directions for goal setting research. *European Psychologist, 12*(4), 290–300.

Lee, V. E., & Smith, J. B. (1996). Collective responsibility for learning and its effects on gains in achievement for early secondary school students. *American Journal of Education, 104*(2), 103–147.

Leithwood, K., Day, C., Sammons, P., Harris, A., & Hopkins, D. (2006). *Seven strong claims about successful school leadership.* Nottingham, UK: National College of School Leadership.

Leithwood, K., Harris, A., & Hopkins, D. (2008). Seven strong claims about successful school leadership. *School Leadership & Management, 28*(1), 27–42.

Leithwood, K., & Steinbach, R. (1995). *Expert problem solving: Evidence from school and district leaders.* Albany: State University of New York Press.

Levin, B. (2008). *How to change 5000 schools: A practical and positive approach for leading change at every level.* Cambridge, MA: Harvard Education Press.

Lipka, J., Hogan, M. P., Webster, J. P., Yanez, E., Adams, B., Clark, S., et al. (2005). Math in a cultural context: Two case studies of a successful culturally based math project. *Anthropology and Education Quarterly, 36*(4), 367–385.

Lipman, P. (1997). Restructuring in context: A case study of teacher participation and the dynamics of ideology, race, and power. *American Educational Research Journal, 34,* 3–28.

Louden, W., & Wildy, H. (1999). Short shrift to long lists: An alternative approach to the development of performance standards for school principals. *Journal of Educational Administration, 37,* 99–120.

Louis, K. S., Leithwood, K., Wahlstrom, K., & Anderson, S. E. (2010). Unpublished interview data from *Learning from leadership: Investigating the links to improved student learning.* Minneapolis: University of Minnesota and the Wallace Foundation.

Marks, H. M., & Printy, S. M. (2003). Principal leadership and school performance: An integration of transformational and instructional leadership. *Educational Administration Quarterly, 39*(3), 370–397.

Marzano, R. J., Waters, T., & McNulty, B. (2005). *School leadership that works: From research to results*. Aurora, CO: ASCD and McREL.

Matsumura, L. C., Sartoris, M., Bickel, D. D., & Garnier, H. E. (2009). Leadership for literacy coaching: The principal's role in launching a new coaching program. *Educational Administration Quarterly, 45*(5), 655–693.

Mayer, R., & Moreno, R. (2003). Nine ways to reduce cognitive load in multimedia learning. *Educational Psychologist, 38*(1), 43–52.

Mercado, C. I. (2001). The learner: Race, ethnicity and linguistic difference. In V. Richardson (Ed.), *The handbook of research on teaching* (4th ed., pp. 668–694). Washington, DC: American Educational Research Association.

Miles, K. H., & Frank, S. (2008). *The strategic school: Making the most of people, time and money*. Thousand Oaks, CA: Corwin Press.

Mintrop, H., & Sunderman, G. L. (2009). Predictable failure of federal sanctions-driven accountability for school improvement—And why we may retain it anyway. *Educational Researcher, 38*(5), 353–364.

Mintzberg, H. (2009). *Managing*. San Francisco: Berrett-Koehler.

Nelson, B. S., & Sassi, A. (2005). *The effective principal: Instructional leadership for high quality learning*. New York: Teachers College Press.

Newmann, F. (1994). *School-wide professional community: Issues in restructuring schools* (Issue Report no. 6, p. 2). Madison: Center on Organization and Restructuring of Schools, University of Wisconsin.

Newmann, F. M., Smith, B., Allensworth, E., & Bryk, A. S. (2001). Instructional program coherence: What it is and why it should guide school improvement policy. *Educational Evaluation and Policy Analysis, 23*(4), 297–321.

New Zealand Ministry of Education. (2007). *The New Zealand curriculum for English-medium teaching and learning Years 1–13*. Wellington, NZ: Author.

New Zealand Ministry of Education. (2008). *Kiwi leadership for principals: Principals as educational leaders*. Wellington, NZ: Author.

Nuthall, G. (2000). The anatomy of memory in the classroom: Understanding how students acquire memory processes from classroom activities in science and social studies units. *American Educational Research Journal, 37*(1), 274–304.

Nuthall, G. (2007). *The hidden lives of learners*. Wellington, NZ: NZCER Press.

Nuthall, G., & Alton-Lee, A. (1993). Predicting learning from student experience of teaching: A theory of student knowledge construction in classrooms. *American Educational Research Journal, 30*, 799–840.

Odden, A. R. (2009). *10 strategies for doubling student performance*. Thousand Oaks, CA: Corwin Press.

Odden, A. R., & Archibald, S. (2001). *Reallocating resources: How to boost student achievement without spending more*. Thousand Oaks, CA: Corwin Press.

O'Shaughnessy, J. (Ed.). (2007). *The leadership effect: Can headteachers make a difference?* London: Policy Exchange.

Paas, F., Renkl, A., & Sweller, J. (2003). Cognitive load theory and instructional design: Recent developments. *Educational Psychologist, 38*(1), 1–4.

Pajak, E., & Arrington, A. (2004). Empowering a profession: Rethinking the roles of administrative evaluation and instructional supervision in improving teacher quality. In M. A. Smylie & D. Miretzky (Eds.), *Developing the teacher workforce (103rd yearbook of the National Society for the Study of Education)* (pp. 228–253). Chicago: National Society for the Study of Education.

Park, V. (2008). *Beyond the numbers chase: How urban high school teachers make sense of data use* (Unpublished doctoral dissertation). University of Southern California, San Diego.

Park, V., & Datnow, A. (2009). Co-constructing distributed leadership: District and school connections in data-driven decision making. *School Leadership & Management, 29*(5), 477–494.

Patall, E. A., Cooper, H., & Robinson, J. C. (2008). Parent involvement in homework: A research synthesis. *Review of Educational Research, 78*(4), 1039–1101.

Reeves, D. B. (2009). *Assessing educational leaders: Evaluating performance for improved individual and organizational results*. Thousand Oaks, CA: Corwin Press.

Riley, K. A. (2007). *Surviving and thriving as an urban leader*. London: Institute of Education.

Rivkin, S. G., Hanushek, E. A., & Kain, J. F. (2005). Teachers, schools and academic achievement. *Econometrica, 72*(2), 417–458.

Robinson, V.M.J. (2001). Embedding leadership in task performance. In K. Wong & C. Evers (Eds.), *Leadership for quality schooling: International perspectives* (pp. 90–102). London: Falmer Press.

Robinson, V.M.J. (2006). Putting education back into educational leadership. *Leading & Managing, 12*(1), 62–75.

Robinson, V.M.J., Hohepa, M., & Lloyd, C. (2009). *School leadership and student outcomes: Identifying what works and why*. Wellington: New Zealand Ministry of Education. Retrieved from www.educationcounts.govt.nz/publications/series/2515/60169/60170.

Robinson, V.M.J., Lloyd, C., & Rowe, K. J. (2008). The impact of leadership on student outcomes: An analysis of the differential effects of leadership type. *Educational Administration Quarterly, 44*(5), 635–674.

Robinson, V.M.J., Phillips, G., & Timperley, H. (2002). Using achievement data for school-based curriculum review: A bridge too far? *Leadership and Policy in Schools, 1*(1), 3–29.

Robinson, V.M.J., & Timperley, H. (2007). The leadership of the improvement of teaching and learning: Lessons from initiatives with positive outcomes for students. *Australian Journal of Education, 51*(3), 247–262.

Rorrer, A. K., & Skrla, L. (2005). Leaders as policy mediators: The reconceptualization of accountability. *Theory into Practice, 44*(1), 53–62.

Scheerens, J., & Bosker, R. (1997). *The foundations of educational effectiveness.* Oxford, UK: Pergamon Press.

Scriven, M. (1990). Can research-based teacher evaluation be saved? *Journal of Personnel Evaluation in Education, 4*(1), 19–32.

Seddon, J. (2008). *Systems thinking in the public sector.* Axminster, UK: Triarchy Press.

Seijts, G. H., & Latham, G. P. (2005). Learning versus performance goals: When should each be used? *Academy of Management Executive, 19*(1), 124–131.

Sharkey, N. S., & Murnane, R. J. (2006). Tough choices in designing a formative assessment system. *American Journal of Education, 112*(4), 572–588.

Sheldon, S. B. (2003). Linking school, family, and community partnerships in urban elementary schools to student achievement on state tests. *Urban Review, 35*(2), 149–165.

Sheldon, S. B. (2005). Testing a structural equation model of partnership program implementation and parent involvement. *Elementary School Journal, 106*(2), 171–187.

Sheldon, S. B., & Van Voorhis, F. E. (2004). Partnership programs in U.S schools: Their development and relationship to family involvement outcomes. *School Effectiveness & School Improvement, 15*(2), 125–145.

Skrla, L., Scheurich, J. J., & Johnson, J. F. (2000). *Equity-driven achievement-focused school districts: A report on systemic school success in four Texas school districts serving diverse student populations.* Austin: Charles A. Dana Center, University of Texas at Austin.

Slavin, R. E., Cheung, A., Groff, C., & Lake, C. (2008). Effective reading programs for middle and high schools: A best-evidence synthesis. *Reading Research Quarterly, 43*(3), 290–322.

Slavin, R. E., Lake, C., Chambers, B., Cheung, A., & Davis, S. (2009). Effective reading programs for the elementary grades. *Review of Educational Research, 79*(4), 1391–1466.

Smylie, M. A., & Bennett, A. (2005). What do we know about developing school leaders? A look at existing research and next steps for new study. In W. A. Firestone & C. Riehl (Eds.), *A new agenda for research in educational leadership* (pp. 138–155). New York: Teachers College Press.

Spillane, J. P. (2006). *Distributed leadership*. San Francisco: Jossey-Bass.

Spillane, J. P., Reiser, B. J., & Reimer, T. (2002). Policy implementation and cognition: Reframing and refocusing implementation research. *Review of Educational Research, 72*, 387–431.

Spillane, J. P., & Seashore Louis, K. (2002). School improvement process and practices: Professional learning for building instructional capacity. In J. Murphy (Ed.), *The educational leadership challenge: Redefining leadership for the 21st century* (pp. 83–104). Chicago: University of Chicago Press.

Stein, M. K., & Nelson, B. S. (2003). Leadership content knowledge. *Educational Evaluation and Policy Analysis, 25*, 423–448.

Stone, D., Patton, B., & Heen, S. (2000). *Difficult conversations*. London: Penguin Books.

Timperley, H. (2005a). Distributed leadership: Developing theory from practice. *Journal of Curriculum Studies, 37*(4), 395–420.

Timperley, H. (2005b). Instructional leadership challenges: The case of using student achievement information for instructional improvement. *Leadership and Policy in Schools, 4*(1), 3–22.

Timperley, H. (2008). *Teacher professional learning and development* (Vol. 18). Brussels: International Academy of Education and International Bureau of Education.

Timperley, H., & Alton-Lee, A. (2008). Reframing teacher professional learning: An alternative policy approach to strengthening valued outcomes for diverse learners. In G. Kelly, A. Luke, & J. Green (Eds.), *Review of research in education* (Vol. 32, pp. 328–369). Thousand Oaks, CA: Sage.

Timperley, H., Smith, L., Parr, J., Portway, J., Mirams, S., Clark, S., et al. (2004). *Analysis and use of student achievement data (AUSAD): Final evaluation report prepared for the Ministry of Education*. Wellington: New Zealand Ministry of Education. Retrieved from www.educationcounts.govt.nz/publications/schooling/5023

Tschannen-Moran, M., & Hoy, W. K. (2000). A multidisciplinary analysis of the nature, meaning, and measurement of trust. *Review of Educational Research, 70*(4), 547–593.

Tymms, P. (2004). Are standards rising in English primary schools? *British Educational Research Journal, 30*(4), 477–494.

Voss, J. F. (1989). Problem-solving and the educational process. In A. Lesgold & K. Glaser (Eds.), *Foundations for a psychology of education* (pp. 251–294). Hillsdale, NJ: Lawrence Erlbaum.

Wang, M.-T., & Holcombe, R. (2010). Adolescents' perceptions of school environment, engagement and academic achievement in middle school. *American Educational Research Journal, 47*(3), 633–662.

Wayman, J. C., & Stringfield, S. (2006). Technology-supported involvement of entire faculties in examination of student data for instructional improvement. *American Journal of Education, 112*(4), 549–571.

Yariv, E. (2009). The appraisal of teachers' performance and its impact on the mutuality of principal-teacher emotions. *School Leadership & Management, 29*(5), 445–461.

Index

Page references followed by *fig* indicate an illustrated figure; followed by *t* indicate a table.